M

THE BIG PICTURE

Other titles by William Goldman published by Applause Books:

WILLIAM GOLDMAN: FIVE SCREENPLAYS
With Essays
All the President's Men • Harper • Magic • The Great Waldo Pepper • Maverick

WILLIAM GOLDMAN: FOUR SCREENPLAYS
With Essays
Butch Cassidy and the Sundance Kid • Marathon Man • The Princess Bride • Misery

ABSOLUTE POWER
By William Goldman, with Introductory Essay

THE GHOST AND THE DARKNESS
By William Goldman, with Introductory Essay

All Goldman titles:
100 PERCENT OF AUTHOR ROYALTIES DONATED TO THE MOTION PICTURE AND TELEVISION FUND

THE BIG PICTURE

Who Killed Hollywood?
and Other Essays

WILLIAM GOLDMAN

APPLAUSE
NEW YORK • LONDON

The Big Picture
An Applause Original
© William Goldman, 2000
All Rights Reserved.

Library of Congress Cataloging-in-Publication Data

Library of Congress Card Number: 99-068321

British Cataloging in Publication Data
A catalogue record of this book is available from the British Library

APPLAUSE BOOKS

1841 Broadway
Suite 1100
New York, NY 10023
Phone (212) 765-7880
Fax: (212) 765-7875

PRINTED IN CANADA

Combined Book Services Ltd.
Units I/K Paddock Wood Dist. Ctr.
Paddock Wood,
Tonbridge Kent TN12 6UU
Phone 0189 283-7171
Fax 0189 283-7272

For The Kids

Contents

I'm Going to Put Your
Head Between Your Ears!

The reason this book exists has nothing to do with Hollywood—it's a jagged line, half a century long, beginning with an uncle's passion, an afternoon with Bronko Nagurski, two phone calls, a divorce, and here we are.

Nothing comes from nothing and trying to write this, I went wriggling back through time and who should be waiting there for me but Uncle Victor. What a surprise to see him again, because he has been dead for many years, and we were never close. He was loud and when I was six and seven and eight, frightening. Usually when we met in those years he would grab my head and shake it, shouting '**I'm going to put your head between your ears!**' and for the longest time, I wondered if anybody could be brave enough to survive such pain. The day I realized my head *was* between my ears was the first step toward my realizing that for all his noise and bluster, I could put away my fears. He was, at heart, a dear, sweet man.

But that is not necessarily a formula for worldly success. School didn't interest him so he didn't stay in it very long; business caused problems too, and for awhile, he came to live in my

mother's house with me. By now, disappointment was wallpa-
pered on; his energy level, always so high, was only an occasional flicker. For all our proximity, we did not bond. He
drifted away, we lost touch, I came to New York, he died. But
by then the seed was planted.

Because Uncle Victor was a sports nut. (Please do
not throw the book across the room—I promise we'll eventually get to Southern California.)

This is Chicago now, starting around the late thirties
and my father, a distant figure in my life, crucial, of course, but
not warm, had sons, my late brother Jim (*The Lion in Winter*,
fabulous) four years older, and me. Victor had a lot of drive in
those years, enough to pull my father along, to get him out of
the house with his children. And so, from when I was very
young, I got to tag along, saw such wonders.

DiMaggio lining a winning double off Comiskey's left
field wall and I still remember the wide-legged stance. (I was
six that day and he was all of twenty-two.) I saw Louis old and
Robinson when he was still young enough to be the greatest
fighter who ever lived. The phrase 'pound for pound' was invented for him.

And of course, I saw the Bears. Uncle Victor had season tickets starting (I think) when the Bears started, mid-twen-
ties. Later, we got tickets too, and I got to watch the Monsters
of the Midway, starting in 1940, attending faithfully till I left for
college, a decade later. This, the first great football dynasty,
popularized the T formation, had many great players, Luckman
and Turner and 'One play' McAfee.

Plus, for a single season only, the mighty Bronko,
Nagurski himself.

And when I die if you ask me the single most exciting
thing I ever saw in my life on earth I would say it was the af-

ternoon when the ancient Nagurski, six years retired, came slowly off the bench and carried us to the championship. I have written that story more often than any other, I suppose, still haven't gotten it right, but that doesn't mean I'm finished trying.

OK. I became a sports nut too. Everything except hockey. (You don't want to know how much time I spend reading sports sections.) I knew early on I wanted to write and in those years, what I wanted to be was a newspaper columnist, John P. Carmichael, Arch Ward, all my other childhood stars.

Never happened. I think because the urge to report about sports was overtaken by the urge to try and tell stories of my own, even though in those early years, no one who knew me was betting heavily in my favor.

In 1956, at twenty four, I wrote my first novel, *The Temple of Gold*; Knopf published it the next year so my sports fantasies went into the drawer since I was suddenly, shockingly, a novelist.

The first phone call, referred to at the start, came thirty years later, from Mike Lupica. He was, for me, then as now, the best sports columnist in the business. I followed his work for years before I ever met him. He said this to me that January day: 'why don't we write a sports book together?'

Wait Till Next Year was published in 1988, and no, you haven't heard of it, but it was a wonderful experience. Many reasons—I had someone else along. So I couldn't take all the blame. The book was about sports in New York, from differing points of view, the reporter and the fan. I got to write about my Knicks—I was already a season ticker holder so what could be better than that? I'll tell you—

—**press passes.**

I got to go to Shea and Yankee Stadium and sit in the

press box with real reporters. I was back in my childhood fantasy now, listening to them talk, finding out some of what they knew that of course they could not write.

The second phone call was from Ed Kosner, then the respected and funny editor of *New York* magazine—it's 1989. He asked what I would think about writing for *New York* and I said that I had never done magazine work, what would I write about and he said well, did you like writing about sports and I said sure and he said, you could write about that for us. Then he added this: "You could write about Hollywood too. Whatever you want, the Oscars maybe, stars, what's going on Out There." I thanked him, and said I would think about it, but in truth, the odds were against accepting. Until he said these magic words:

"I can get you press passes."

So back I went, and for years to come, to the ball games and the writers and the food—neither team's worth a star but so what, I loved it, and you don't know why—*I wasn't alone.*

Because during this time, my in all ways splendid wife of thirty years couldn't take it anymore, (never blamed her) and I was suddenly just another middle-aged bachelor in the city who had not dated in a *very* long time. The best stat I could come up with was this: *I had not dated since before the Beatles went to Germany.*

And I was scared, don't you see, how the world had changed since the Eisenhower era and the loneliness lurking out there in the dark, but when the clouds began to gather, I had my fix—subway to the Bronx, taxi out to Shea.

This book exists then for primarily one reason: it helped me to keep the demons at bay.

What you have here is a chronicle of the worst decade in movie history. If you were to ask me what were the ten best films of the 90's my first thought would be of the old joke 'the girls in my town were so ugly that once we had a beauty contest and nobody won.'

Shawshank Redemption, that I know. And *Unforgiven*, *Babe*, and *Hoop Dreams*. *Fargo*, absolutely. *What's Eating Gilbert Grape?* Think so. Yes to *Four Weddings and A Funeral*. Have to see *Groundhog Day* again. I'm sure there are others but it's tough sledding from then on. For me, anyway. I hope you had a better time.

The book is primarily about what Hollywood is primarily about—stars, money and for one night only (Oscar night) quality.

Going backwards, as you will find, I am one of those who feels these two things about the Oscars: the show is always too short and, more importantly, it is *nuts* they don't let us know the votes.

I always enjoyed those articles because, as we all know, there is no 'best' anything, only what we favor.

But you cannot imagine what it would have been like for me to write about the awards of 25 years ago. These are the 1975 Best Picture Nominees:

Barry Lyndon

Dog Day Afternoon

. *Jaws*

Nashville

One Flew Over the Cuckoo's Nest

Not a fluke. Let me go back twenty-five additional years. Here are ten flicks that did *not* get Best Picture nominations for 1950.

Annie Get Your Gun

Asphalt Jungle

Broken Arrow

Caged

Cinderella

The Gunfighter

The Men

No Way Out

Panic in the Streets

The Third Man

The point is not that these got robbed. (I could easily throw in ten others.) It's just to show what Hollywood was turning out once. It's not the number of glories, it's the overall depth of quality. (To put you out of your misery, the best flicks were:)

All About Eve

Born Yesterday

Father of the Bride

King Solomon's Mines

Sunset Boulevard

Two out of five masterpieces, not so terrible.

Have there been that many this entire decade?

Not to drive you nuts with names, but sure, '50 was a swell year. But not in a class with the year that followed. Here are best pictures, 1951:

An American in Paris

Decision Before Dawn

A Place in the Sun

Quo Vadis

A Streetcar Named Desire

Three greats out of five. Three flicks they still show today that thrill audiences. Houston, Kazan, Minnelli, Stevens and Wyler got directing nominations.

But Hitchcock didn't and he had *Strangers on a Train*, and Wilder didn't and all he gave us was *The Big Carnival*.

Talk about actors? Arthur Kennedy got nominated, *Bright Victory*. Fine fine actor, got five nominations in all, never quite won. Frederick March got nominated for *Death of a Salesman*. March, great on both stage and screen, won two best actor awards. Know who the other three guys were? Three of the greatest performers of the century. Bogart, Brando and Clift. In three of their greatest performances, *The African Queen, A Place in the Sun, A Streetcar Named Desire.*

How great to write about that year, those guys.

(I realize I've just segued from Oscars to stars, but before I get there, a quick word about money.)

These are terrible times in the movie business. Hard to believe that because, as I write this, the summer of '99 has been so big at the box office. *Wild Wild West*, for example, has passed a hundred million. Good for Warner Brothers, the studio that financed it, right? Maybe, maybe not. Because there are rumors—hotly denied as they always say—that this baby may have cost close to *two hundred million dollars*. Scary.

But it's not out there all by it's lonesome. Costs are out of control, and getting increasingly so; the studios are slashing producer deals in an effort to save money. It costs twenty-five million dollars just to open a picture that first weekend nowadays. (And that's on the low side.) Paramount was recently derided when it wanted co-financing. Just about everyone is doing it now.

Ask anyone in the movie business that isn't a flack or a hack and they will sing the same song, and it's not some sappy ballad. In Hollywood right now, the Blues have control.

Ok, on to the good stuff, stars.

One of the exercises you'll find in these essays is trying to figure out just who is the biggest star in the world. What I found fascinating was everything seems so sure and solid concerning stars, if we read the media. In truth, all and always quicksilver.

So now, dear reader, on this, the afternoon of the 16th of July, 1999 I am going to ask you this question: **who is the biggest star in the world?**

Take a second and think about it. There is, obviously, no right answer but you can circle in on certain names. It is no longer Arnold. Not Kevin. They are both very much around, will be in many more hits; but I doubt even their agents would claim their guy was numero uno.

Here's a guy who has to be named first: Will Smith. Last three flicks, *Enemy of the State, Men in Black, Independence Day*. Wherever *Wild Wild West* ends up, here's a stat for you: these four flicks will average a box office gross over *200 million dollars per picture*. Hard to argue against Will Smith.

Excuuuuuse me? This from the Carrey camp. The last five years, these: *Ace Ventura, Pet Detective, The Mask, Dumb and Dumber, Batman Forever, Ace Ventura: When Nature Calls, The*

Cable Guy, Liar, Liar, The Truman Show. (For which he was now and forever robbed of an Oscar nomination. And while I'm here, let me say that giving the Best Actor - **actor** is the word folks—to Roberto Benigni for his mugging in *Life is Beautiful* is for me, a sin, a disgrace, and removes forever the argument from those who felt DeMille's *Greatest Show on Earth* was the worst Oscar winner ever. I was at Cannes when Benigni got an award there and you know that cute/bullshit/what language is that? speech he gave at the Oscars? He's got a patent on it.) I have also read Jim Carrey's summer movie, *Me Myself and Irene*, by the Farrelly Brothers, and it is going to be as big as anything Carrey's ever done. (And leave us not forget *Man in the Moon*, directed by double Oscar Winner Milos Forman, due later this year.) I think it's impossible to argue against Jim Carrey.

But what about the older (joke—read more mature) guys like Mel Gibson? *Braveheart, Ransom, Lethal*s '94 and '95? Among others hits. Nobody beats Mel.

Unless it's TC. Last five Tom Cruise flicks:

A Few Good Men

The Firm

Interview With the Vampire

Mission: Impossible

Jerry Maguire

I think that is a Hollywood record—five consecutive films each grossing more than one hundred million dollars. No star *ever* did that. It is inconceivable to go against Tom—and he's nice *and* he's just 37.

But Tom Hanks is star of the decade.

A League of Their Own

Sleepless in Seattle

Philadelphia

Forrest Gump

Apollo 13

You've Got Mail

Saving Private Ryan

Not just hits, not just terrific flicks, but most of them Oscar contenders and none of them huge special effects summer stuff. Here's something I know you soon will—Hanks' next may be his best, *The Green Mile*. I have read Frank Darabont's script and it is sensational. The word on the movie is already big and building.

Ok. Reader, time to suck it up. Here they are again, this time billing alphabetical.

Carrey

Cruise

Gibson

Hanks

Smith

Remember again, no right answer. But look at it logically. Then decide. Got your guy?

Well you are wrong!

At this time in world history, we all inhabit a planet in which the biggest star is . . . wait for it . . . yes I'm serious, . . . **Adam Sandler.**

(Whew.)

I talked to a top studio guy today and he said this: "You can absolutely make a case for Adam Sandler being *the* star. His movies cost next to zero and bring in a ton. Huge profits. Isn't that what a star's supposed to do?"

The point of this is just to say to remind you how fast it changes.

This year has been remarkable in that *four* new stars have exploded in the first six months: Reeves and Fraser and Myers and Sandler. First time since '94 anything like that happened. (And this year's only half over.)

I want to talk about the new stars of '94—not so very long ago, let's remind ourselves, and track what has become of them. Remember always that studios *need* stars. And that a star is not held responsible for the ultimate fate of a film, but only *that first weekend*. A star must *open* a picture.

Hugh Grant came first in '94. March of that year, *Four Weddings and A Funeral.* Seven years in pictures, starting with *Maurice* in '87. Full disclosure: I know Grant, like him, have worked with him. But the biggest hit he has had since '94 was this summer's *Notting Hill.* My feeling is he is still very much a star, probably now the most sought after romantic comedy lead, along with Tom Hanks. But the public has not embraced him in other roles. So he is what he was; certainly has not fallen, probably has not climbed.

Keanu Reeves came next, June, in *Speed.* But he was never quite believed Out There, and some of his ensuing choices—*A Walk in the Clouds, Feeling Minnesota,* made few hearts go pitty-pat. He was suddenly gone again. It was almost as if '94 hadn't happened. Then *Devil's Advocate* did business. And now with *The Matrix,* he is a locomotive. Much bigger than he was. And the feeling is, apt to remain so.

July brought *The Mask.* (*Ace Ventura, Pet Detective* came earlier that year, but no one quite realized what Jim Carrey was till this baby.) He has not looked back since '94 and *Cable Guy,* which a lot of media claimed to be a stiff, made money—so did *Striptease*, another media 'disaster.' Carrey is the comedy star of the decade.

Tim Allen arrived for Christmas. *The Santa Clause* began his film career, but where has he gone since? *Jungle2Jungle* and not a lot else. I think, with his TV series gone, he has done the least with his shot at stardom, has the farthest to go to get back. (Unless of course, his next movie is a hit.) A lot of Hollywood folks are surprised by Allen's trajectory—back then, when he happened, the feeling was he was special, and would be with us for a very long time.

Brad Pitt, the fifth star of that year, had a double-hitter, *Interview with the Vampire* and *Legends of the Fall*. He had *Seven* a year later, but his recent choices have been shall we say, commercially shaky. *7 Years In Tibet*, *Devil's Own*, *Meet Joe Black*. Maybe a quarter of a billion down the tubes with that trio.

Still, he is as in demand as ever. And I promise you his price has not gone down. Why you may ask?

For that answer, we have to enter the world of sex. Sometimes beautiful young men are ordained stars by the studios. Whether their record deserves it or not. Guys who *look* like stars.

Example, Richard Gere: made a tremendous impression in 1977. *Looking For Mr. Goodbar*. Gere was anointed. New star. Four straight flops. (Remember please, this is not about the quality of the films or his skill as a performer. This is about opening flicks.) Finally, *Officer and a Gentleman*. See, the execs said? We told you so. Do we know magic or do we know magic?

After *Officer and a Gentleman*, Gere went into a truly phenomenal decline. I am going to list his next seven movies over the next six years. Raise you hands not if you saw these, but if you even *heard* of them.

1983: *Beyond the Limit*

1983: *Breathless*

1984: *The Cotton Club*

1985: *King David*

1986: *No Mercy*

1986: *Power*

1988: *Miles From Home*

Then, in 1990, *Internal Affairs* did some business and *Pretty Woman* made the executives breathe easy again.

More briefly now, another example, Mel Gibson. Sensational in *Mad Max*, 1979. The same in the sequel, *Mad Max 2*, (*Road Warrior* here.)

Another natural, the execs told us. Gibson had four movies in the mid 80's that will not make anybody's Desert Island list: *The Year of Living Dangerously*, *The Bounty*, *Mrs. Soffel*, *The River*. Even the third *Mad Max* was a disappointment. But he was a star, the studios knew it, they kept giving him lead parts in expensive pictures which failed. Then the first *Lethal Weapon* saved his career.

Point being: no female star would have been given so many chances.

Example: everybody's favorite (she is mine) Rene Russo.

1992: *Lethal Weapon 3*

1993: *In the Line of Fire*

1995: *Outbreak*

1995: *Get Shorty*

1996: *Tin Cup*

1997: *Ransom*

Granted, she wasn't the vehicle role, but she was pretty crucial to the successes of those films, don't you think? I do. Six straight hits, five of them (I thought *Outbreak* sucked) terrific entertainments.

OK. 1997 and she finally gets to play the lead. *Buddy*. Didn't work. Guess what? No more vehicle parts. No breaks like Gere got or Gibson got. She is now co-starring again, *The Thomas Crown Affair*. And if it's a big hit? I still think they'll be reluctant to give her another vehicle role.

But Brad Pitt sure will get them. His summer picture of this year, *The Fight Club*, was yanked from the schedule. We'll learn in the fall just why. Was it fear of Littleton because of its violence or were we meeting *Joe Black* again? Doesn't matter to Pitt's career. He is a star. He looks like one. (I happen to think he's terrific. But that's not what we're talking about.) He will go on getting leads—as long as stays beautiful. Of course, if he gains thirty pounds, over and out.

You may know why there are so few female stars. Best I can come up with is simple: guys run the Hollywood show. And guys don't really want women to be stars.

Closing up shop now. What follows is in chronological order and I would guess I get increasingly depressed as the years went on. I have changed nothing, not a word, so all my errors, omissions, and repetitions will be right there for you to see.

A few final reminders. Remember that Hollywood makes no sense. Remember everybody powerful wants to stay powerful, everybody else is out to kill. Remember that movies began—really—as entertainment for illiterates.

How far have we come this first century?

Over to you . . .

THE VOICE OF THE TURTLES

HOW DOES A HIT MOVIE HAPPEN?

Mid-morning, and about a dozen of them stalked the theater lobby. Not much talk; the time for that was done. Outside—perfect December. Inside, pacing and cigarettes. They all smoked. But everybody smoked then, 31 years ago, especially people with pressure jobs, such as these folk, the top of the ad and publicity departments of 20th-Century Fox. A movie was opening in half an hour, here at a 3,650-seat Broadway glory, a true Picture Palace.

The movie was big, too. Gregory Peck opposite Deborah Kerr, playing Scott Fitzgerald and Sheilah Graham in *Beloved Infidel.* That first show would tell so much, all of it summed up in one sentence: *Does the public want to see the picture?* You can test and prod and ask and scuffle, but until it's playing where Just Plain Folk can pay or not, it's all a guess.

They were guessing in the lobby, these dozen executives. No one expected a full house. If 750 people meandered out of the sunshine, they were golden. What would that have meant? Hollywood's three favorite syllables—*blockbuster.*

They looked at their watches. Time. The theater was unlocked, doors opened, admission booths manned.

Four people bought tickets.

Reeling and ashen, one flack turned to another and said these now famous words: "How do they know?"

In the movie business, as it's often been said, nobody knows anything, so don't search for an answer here. But that question is what makes the movies, at least in one crucial way, better than Broadway: With the exception of the frail or the foreign, films don't need critics. Word of mouth is what matters, and the miracle—not too strong a word—is that no one has been able to figure out how to fake it or will it into being.

It's not that the studios don't want to solve the mystery. They commission studies, do surveys. My favorite? The studio that did a survey for a sci-fi flick and discovered there was no audience interest in it whatsoever. So they gave up the picture they had developed. In other words, they *proved* there was no market for *E.T.*

Right now, I truly think Hollywood has the brightest bunch of studio talent in the quarter-century I've been in the screen trade. These are outstanding executives; yet in the past months, four movies have been released, blockbusters all, and every major studio passed on all of them.

Take the case of Amy Heckerling. She had a notion for a romantic film with a kicker: The baby in the movie not only could understand what the adults were doing but could comment on their behavior. Sorry, said the majors.

Eventually, Tri-Star, which had produced an amazing string of clinkers, got involved. *Look Who's Talking* stars the all-but-interred John Travolta and TV's Kirstie Alley as the grown-ups, while Bruce Willis supplies the child's chitchat.

By the time the movie was done, a new overall executive had been temporarily ensconced, who decided that the movie could not be advertised easily and, as a result, settled on a regional release pattern, saving money. *Look Who's Talking* would open in the states of Oregon and Washington. And if it did well, in other areas. If not, it would never be shown.

The movie was suddenly a whisper away from oblivion, because it is doubtful that it would have found an audience in those two states, with no hot stars and a limited advertising budget. Fire storm at Tri-Star. Wires and letters, shouts and begging. Pressure is put on the new head, who finally, grudgingly succumbs.

Look Who's Talking will take in $140 million at American box-offices. A sequel and a TV series are in the works.

When a hit happens, the studios immediately grab the lead, so I asked an executive, "Is John Travolta now the hottest star?"

He said, "Some warmth, yes, but not all that much—we don't feel he was the reason for the success of the picture."

I said I thought Travolta was charming and winning and was, after all, the lead.

"It wasn't him, believe me."

"Then what?"

"The voice of Bruce Willis," he said. Understand—this is not a dumb guy.

"Explain to me," I said, "if the *voice* of Bruce Willis is worth over a hundred million at the box-office, how is *all* of Bruce Willis, with the best reviews of his career, dying with *In Country?*"

The executive got angry. "If you're not going to try and

make sense, there's no point to carrying on this conversation."

Driving Miss Daisy was rejected by everybody when the budget was $12.5 million, cheap for a major Hollywood film. Re-thinking followed. The producers tried again, this time with a budget of $7.5 million. Total rejection. The thinking? It probably would make a nice little picture. It might even win a couple of minor prizes. But no one would venture near the theaters.

Richard Zanuck, one of the producers, couldn't quite believe the reaction. And Richard Zanuck knows Hollywood. Child of Darryl, he's been deeply involved with *The Sting, Jaws, The Verdict,* and *Cocoon,* among other movies. "It got so embarrassing," he said. "I was getting turned down by companies I'd never heard of. I got so where I wanted to quit."

He didn't, and if you saw the Oscars, you know it all had a happy Hollywood ending. *Daisy* will end up as one of the most successful dramas ever.

But, Zanuck feels, it won't change a thing. The next time he or anybody else goes out with an offbeat film, the struggle will start again. The studio heads today are smarter, yes, but they're also businessmen, who rely on market research. "You ask in a mall if anyone wants to see a movie starring Morgan Freeman and Jessica Tandy, they're going to say no. There are no passionate guys in the top jobs. If you try again and mention *Daisy* as an example of an offbeat picture that worked, they'll just dismiss it as another nonrecurring phenomenon."

At one point, Zanuck was meeting with a European-born executive who knew that *Daisy* was the story of 25 years in the relationship of an elderly black chauffeur and an even older white woman. "I think you're not thinking big enough," the man said. "I think we are talking here about a *hundred-million-dollar movie.*" Zanuck was stunned.

"Let me say two words to you," the executive went on.

Zanuck sat quietly. There was a long pause. Then the two words were spoken: "Eddie Murphy."

The screenplay *Three Thousand*, by Jonathan Lawton, had been around for several years, seen by all, embraced by no one. A small, dark film about a rich guy and a whore, it was an anti-Cinderella tale in which the guy takes up with the hooker and eventually dumps her.

Enter Disney's Jeffrey Katzenberg. A peer of his says, "We're none of us curing cancer, but if there were a poll out here about who would you most want to run your studio, I'd bet on Jeffrey to win."

At a meeting of Disney executives, Katzenberg asked who had come across anything recently. One young guy said, "I read this script, *Three Thousand*, about a billionaire and a hooker and they have an affair and he buys her nice things, and at the end he dumps her." Someone else said, "Oh, I read that, it's good writing." A third echoed the sentiment.

Katzenberg, who had long wanted to make a movie on the Pygmalion theme, said, "Why does he have to dump her? Why does it have to be unhappy?" Then he added, "We're going to acquire that and change it, and we're going to do it right away."

Casting *Pretty Woman* took a while. There was no major star who was right for the girl, so director Garry Marshall tested several actresses and Julia Roberts was golden.

But the male lead was not so easy. Some acquaintances were casting a romantic movie a year ago. Today, they would have gone after, alphabetically, Michael Douglas, Harrison Ford, and Richard Gere as their top trio. Twelve months past? Their list went in age from Tom Hanks to Paul Newman. Mel Gibson was on it. Hoffman and Hackman. Keaton and

Nicholson. Costner and De Niro. Kurt Russell. Jeff Bridges. Dreyfuss, Hurt, Kevin Kline, Tom Selleck, Steve Martin, Chevy Chase.

And Richard Gere? Why wasn't he there? No one thought to mention his name. Because of flicks you didn't see like *Power* and *The Cotton Club* and *No Mercy*, *Beyond the Limit*, *Miles From Home*. Gere had ceased to exist.

You explain it.

While you're at it, explain *Teenage Mutant Ninja Turtles*, because, as one executive said to me, "I missed it. It's my job to spot trends, and I missed it. I've got little kids. *They* wouldn't have missed it."

We are talking of the greatest freak hit in American movie history. After three days, it was the third fastest-grossing movie ever, behind only *Batman* and *Ghostbusters II*. Those two cost, total, nearly $100 million. *Ninja Turtles* cost maybe ten.

Every major studio passed. Every minor studio passed. Twelve places didn't get it. Why? A lot of people have come up with reasons, but there are two that seem so crazy I believe them.

(1) *It didn't cost enough.*

That isn't a typo. Studios *like* to pay a lot of money. It means they're buying something of value. There's something wrong with a movie like *Ninja Turtles* when it's going to cost you only $10.4 million, the budget when everybody turned away. Movies about comic characters cost 50 plus. *Batman*, *Superman*.

I first came across this kind of reasoning in 1962 when I saw a splendid movie, *Ride the High Country*, which opened to wonderful notices on the bottom half of a double bill. A studio executive I knew explained that *Ride the High Country* had been tested and had done brilliantly. But they didn't believe the test results. "It didn't cost enough to be that good," the studio guy said. Maybe, if the people who had developed *Ninja Turtles* had gone in demanding $50.4 million, they would have found a taker.

(2) *Howard the Duck.*

Ishtar may be the most famous recent megastiff, but even that picture couldn't compete with *Howard the Duck* in one crucial way—Howie cost a studio head his job. There was a famous *Variety* headline that went, 'DUCK' COOKS PRICE'S GOOSE, which meant that Frank Price had been canned from Universal, essentially for the failure of the duck flick. I'd bet that every executive who turned down the turtles paused for a minute, thinking of Price's sad fate. (Not all that sad—Price is now back running Columbia.)

In movie history, there has never been a time as commercially hot as now, in great part because of the films talked about here, all four of which almost never happened. They came from four different studios, but any studio could have banked the quartet.

And if they had? Conservatively? Oh, half a billion dollars. All profit . . . .

—MAY 21, 1990

CHRISTMAS IN JULY

A PREVIEW OF HOLIDAY HOPEFULS

Furriers, glove manufacturers, cloak-and-suiters—these were the men who gave us Hollywood. That much, of course, is commonly known. What isn't is this: The movie business still resembles the clothing business in one essential way—it's seasonal. Just as bathing suits are not much on the mind of Ralph Lauren these days, the summer movies onscreen now are as important to the thinking of the men who run Hollywood as "Will the Mets fire Davey Johnson?"

In other words, the summer pictures—about which you are reading everywhere—are already very ancient history. They are locked in stone, their theaters booked, their ad budgets set. The battleground right now—in July, just as we're getting a decent tan—is Christmas.

And this Christmas—which, for movie purposes, starts at Thanksgiving—is going to be the biggest in the history of Hollywood. "By far the biggest," one executive told me. "*Way* by far."

Also the most expensive. More than a billion dollars

will have been spent to make and market twenty-plus films. A *lot* of money is going to be made.

And lost.

I've talked to a bunch of Hollywood Powers about the Christmas films, asking them which ones they thought would break out, hitting today's magic number—$100 million at the box-office. Since none of the movies is finished, these opinions are based entirely on hunch, gossip, and prayer. I'll talk to these same men again in November, when they've seen the Product, and again in late January, when the results are in and—as one of them put it— "after the blood has been spilled. And are you going to see blood!"

What follows is a listing, alphabetical within category, of the movies that are, as of now, likely to open for the holidays. My arbitrary categories are Sequels, Popular Fare, and Oscar Hopefuls. Not all these movies will actually open during this period—some of them surely must blink. Since the costs have never been remotely this high, the competition has never been this murderous.

SEQUELS

The Godfather, Part III (Paramount): The Nightmare. The one whose travails you cannot help reading about in magazines. There are whispers that it will be the most expensive movie ever made. This one is in more trouble in the media than any flick in memory—except the first *Godfather*. Coppola back directing, Pacino, Keaton, all your favorites, with the Vatican thrown in. I never bet against talent, and I'm not going to here. Neither did the Powers. They think it's going to be huge—$100 million breezing.

But at least a few are hedging because Martin Scorsese

has directed, for pre-holiday release, a gangster epic of his own, *GoodFellas*, starring Robert De Niro. When these two work together—*Taxi Driver, Raging Bull*—sparks fly. One man said, "Personally, I can't wait to see *III*, but I've got to think Paramount would kill to have the Scorsese disappear." Some thought the Scorsese—based on the book *Wiseguy*, by *New York*'s own Nick Pileggi—would take the edge off the Coppola, while others felt it would only whet interest. How many quality gangster epics is too many quality gangster epics?

Look Who's Talking Too (Tri-Star). "The same group of idiots as the last time, only now they've added Roseanne Barr," said another Power. "Do I sound jealous? That's only because I *am* jealous—that it's not my picture."

Predator 2 (Fox). "Who'd want to see a bloodbath," asked another executive, "when we're singing 'Peace on Earth'?"

Rocky, The Final Bell (MGM/UA). "How much life is left in that character? Not to mention that Stallone's a little long in the tooth for a prizefighter. But I guess the longer George Foreman keeps winning, the greater the reality here."

Three Men and a Little Lady (Touchstone). "The one can't-miss movie of the season. Through the roof. Unless it stinks—in which case, it will also go through the roof."

Prevailing wisdom on Sequels: *Three Men and a Little Lady* will be the biggest of the five. But four of the five—leaving out only *Predator 2*—will be successful.

POPULAR FARE

Almost an Angel (Paramount). Paul Hogan, not as Crocodile Dundee.

Edward Scissorhands (Fox). Tim Burton back in action after *Batman*.

Home Alone (Fox). No one knew anything about this except that it's a John Hughes production, and John Hughes productions make money.

Kindergarten Cop (Universal). Arnold Schwarzenegger directed by Ivan Reitman. "I hate the title. I think the title is an affront to the planet Earth," said one man. "I also think it's an amazingly commercial title, and surely that must say something about Western civilization."

Marrying Man (Hollywood). A Neil Simon comedy starring Alec Baldwin and Kim Basinger.

Misery (Columbia). Rob Reiner saying good-bye to comedy for the moment. A famous Stephen King novel. Incredible unanimity about the quality of the screenplay: "The most brilliant adaptation since *Gone With the Wind*." "Awesome writing." "If they get half of what's on paper on film, it will thrill the world." (Aside: These quotes are, alas, total bulls—. I wrote the screenplay. So I do have at least a little insider information on this one, but will say only this: come Christmas, if Kathy Bates isn't a lot better known than she is now, I will be very surprised.)

The Rookie (Warner Bros.). Clint Eastwood teamed with Charlie Sheen.

Nothing But Trouble (Warner Bros.). Chevy Chase, Dan Aykroyd, and John Candy.

Prevailing wisdom on Popular Fare: Only one of the eight will break out—the Schwarzenegger, *Kindergarten Cop*. Get used to that title.

OSCAR HOPEFULS

Avalon (Tri-Star). If *Three Men and a Little Lady* is the leader in popularity, this is for quality. No one doubted it would be an outstanding film. Logical enough, since it was written and directed by Barry Levinson, whose last two movies were *Good Morning, Vietnam* and *Rain Man*. Another plus: It's his third Baltimore picture—the first two were *Diner* and *Tin Men*, totally respected films.

The famous film editor Dede Allen once said something to the effect that every movie has a soft underbelly, and it's the editor's job to try and hide it as much as possible. *Avalon*'s underbelly? "Nobody writes Baltimore like Levinson. I love those first two movies. But nobody came. Personally, I'm going to love *Avalon*. But who else is going to be in the theater?"

Awakenings (Columbia). Penny Marshall's first directing gig since *Big*. With De Niro and Robin Williams. Very Serious Drama. Very Talented People. Underbelly? "Why do I feel queasy? Where does it say she can do drama? Those are two super actors. Why do I wonder about the chemistry?" No one was specific in nailing down possible problems. But most felt more uncertain about this than any of the others in the category.

The Bonfire of the Vanities (Warner Bros.). Based on an unknown novel by Tom Wolfe. Director: Brian De Palma. Stars: Tom Hanks, Bruce Willis, Melanie Griffith. Underbelly: "Everyone will know when this picture hits the theaters. But I've got a million questions. Everyone also knows they've had major script troubles since before the Piltdown man. And, yes, this baby may have more talent than any other. But is De Palma the right director? He did wonderful satiric comedy when he was younger, but the last one was *Hi, Mom!*, and that was twenty years ago. Tom Hanks—major, major talent, no question. But isn't he a decade too young for the lead? Tell me I'm wrong."

Havana (Universal). Sydney Pollack back in the saddle for the first time since *Out of Africa*. Joined by Redford. This is one of the most remarkable and enduring quality teams in movie history. They *acted* together in 1962 (*War Hunt*). Their actor-director association began four years later with *This Property Is Condemned*. They did *Jeremiah Johnson*, one of the great Westerns; *The Way We Were*; half a dozen films—no stiffs. Underbelly? "Isn't it about the fall of Cuba when Castro took over? Do we care about that? I've got bigger problems. What if it opens against *Avalon*? And what if they both go against *Bonfire*? They're all chasing the same grown-up audience, and people just do not skip from theater to theater come Christmas. They might pick one. If God smiles, maybe two. Which?"

The Russia House. Sean and Michelle in the famous Le Carre spy novel. Underbelly? "Did you read that novel? I read that novel. I kept waiting for the story to start, and you know what? It didn't. But it was a big book. Forget my taste. What you can't forget is this: What the hell is it going to be like over there in six months? Of course, if revolution breaks out, that would be good—kidding, kidding."

Scenes From a Mall (Touchstone). Woody Allen and Bette Midler in essentially a two-character movie directed by Paul Mazursky. Underbelly: "The movie of the year I most want to see, and it's not my movie. There's only one problem, and it's this: *Can Woody Allen act?* As Woody Allen—sensational. But the last time he acted, I think, was maybe fifteen years ago, and with a wonderful actor's director, Marty Ritt. *The Front* was the picture. And he stunk. What if he's like that in a two-character picture? If he's great, it'll be great. Vegas should be taking bets on this one."

Prevailing wisdom on the Oscar Hopefuls: All of them will be quality films. None of them will find the audience that, say, *Driving Miss Daisy* did this year.

What we are talking about here—with this glut of expensive and potentially wonderful films all trying to slip through a tiny window—is madness. This isn't summer, when the kids seem as if they're out of school forever—it's essentially Christmas vacation. One studio executive said, "I know it's crazy, but I get caught up in it, too. It's Spago thinking. Everyone sits around and says, 'And what's *your* Christmas picture?' The fact is, we're all afraid to say, 'To hell with Christmas.' "

My view? I think they have to say it eventually, and I believe that this will be the last lunatic Yuletide. *Three* smash hits opened this past March, thought to be a deadly time. Next year, I suspect, March will be much coveted.

Of course, the kids *are* out of school for a while, so there will always be Product. But the price of failure is set so high, I think this stampede has to end. Still, the battle will rage this year as never before—carnage you wouldn't believe when the snow falls.

See you in November . . . .

—JULY 16, 1990

WHITE-KNUCKLE CHRISTMAS

Christmas comes early on the coast. In July, I did a series of interviews with the Hollywood Powers about the 1990 holiday movies—specifically which ones would "break through" at the box-office and pass the sacred $100-million mark. Back then, none of the Mighty had seen anything. But now they have seen a bunch and have read test results on almost all the rest. Their feelings are the same as the last time I spoke with them ("the biggest Christmas in history") and different (some of the July "sure things" are seen to be stumbling). A few facts to help you put things in perspective:

• Almost all movies hit their commercial peak the weekend they open. A falling-off inevitably follows. What makes a great hit is this: a *gradual* falling-off. *Ghost*, already one of the dozen biggest grossers in movie history, opened strongly but not remotely as well as the unlamented "body count" scams of the summer past; i.e., *Another 48 HRS* and *Die Hard 2*. *Ghost* will be more profitable than any two of this year's big-budget flicks put together because it's still out there, whereas Eddie Murphy and Bruce Willis are very long gone.

• Second chances are not to be counted on. (The only exception of the past quarter century might be *Bonnie and Clyde*, which did not do all that well when first released, then ended its run and was shortly put back in release due to the brilliance and pleading of the producer, Mr. Beatty, and went on to justified fame and glory.) In other words, there are no mulligans in movieland.

• The most important fact: At the most, during the holiday season, four movies might break out. But that's rare. Three is more likely. But not certain. In the 1981-1982 season, only one, *On Golden Pond*, was a major hit.

There is always tension in Hollywood. But there is more this year for a remarkable reason. There are not just too many movies opening in too small a window; there are too many *good* pictures.

What follows, as before, is a listing—alphabetically within arbitrary categories—of major studio movies that are going to open between Thanksgiving time and December's end.

SEQUELS

The Godfather, Part III (Paramount). As before, all the pundits felt it would do $100 million. But now, doubts. "Remember, these movies came out in '72 and '74, and they had rich tapestries," said one Power. "They were *stately*. Today's pace is so much faster. Everyone will go that first couple of weeks, but I wouldn't bet on word of mouth." "It will make your so-called magic number, but barely. Could be a big disappointment. Why are they rushing it out?"

This last comment came from everyone. Coppola apparently wanted to wait till Easter. "They got great holiday bookings, but they could have gotten them whenever they opened. I hope I'm wrong, but I've got a feeling that it won't be what it might have been."

Look Who's Talking Too (TriStar). "I thought it would be huge before, but now I'm downgrading. A hit, sure. Seventy-five. The picture isn't ready to open." "Hard to predict on a picture where post-production means so much. All those voices for the kid were what made the first one, and they have to be perfect."

Predator 2 (Twentieth Century Fox). "I thought we were talking disaster here, but now I keep hearing—this from sane people, remember—that the damn thing is *good.*" "I think this is the sleeper of the season because of the monster. It's just a great monster. I'll go out on a limb: It's a franchise monster." (Yes, they do talk that way Out There.)

The Rescuers Down Under (Disney). "It's a cartoon, and they don't do a hundred million. But it's also a Disney cartoon. What do they average—two flops a century? This won't be one of them. A hit in the making."

Rocky V (MGM/UA). "Yeah, yeah, I know, the previews were getting jeered in places. But Stallone's always been controversial. I think it's going to surprise a lot of people because I hear it's not nearly as bad as you might think." "I think it's a rotten idea—the *Rocky* audience is not deeply committed to subtle character development. They want to see a white guy kick some ass—preferably against an ethnic, but a Russian will do fine. If Rocky was fighting a Columbian drug lord, through the roof. But I don't think they're going to line up to see him *teach!*" (This was the only totally negative reaction among the sequels.)

Three Men and a Little Lady (Touchstone). Unanimous. "Blockbuster. Worldwide." "Bigger than the first." "Probably the top commercial movie of the season."

POPULAR FARE

Almost an Angel (Paramount). Unanimous. "Paul Hogan not as Crocodile Dundee? Stiff." "Total Stiff." "Wipeout." "Will get crunched by the competition." Not much hope here from the assembled.

Come See the Paradise (Twentieth Century Fox). "Great . . . just what I want to take the kids to at Christmastime—a Japanese-concentration-camp picture."

Edward Scissorhands (Twentieth Century Fox). Absolute uncertainty. "I know Tim Burton is fresh off *Batman*, but this movie is only testing well with teenage girls. *I* would also like to test well with teenage girls. But I didn't make it, and I don't see this one making it, either." "The left-field sleeper of the season."

Green Card (Touchstone). "It's directed by Peter Weir, so you know it's got quality. But starring Gerard Depardieu? One hundred million? Next case."

Home Alone (Twentieth Century Fox). The unquestionable sleeper of the season. "Another John Hughes hit." "I just keep hearing better and better things about it."

Kindergarten Cop (Universal). "I think it's going to be Arnold's biggest picture." "Huge." "Bigger than huge." "It's between this one and *Three Men* for the championship."

Mermaids (Orion). "Cher's first since *Moonstruck*, and I hear nice." Unanimous feeling that this was one of two that will get killed by the Christmas, competition. "Should have been pushed into spring."

The Rookie (Warner Bros.). "Another Eastwood disappointment." "He's still a great star, but next time he should pick better."

OSCAR HOPEFULS

Alice (Orion). "Woody Allen and Mia and William Hurt and Alec Baldwin, and I think it's going to be terrific. But I'm not sure if all his flicks added together did a hundred at the box."

Awakenings (Columbia). All the Powers I talked to sounded like press agents. "Just a wonderful movie." "Better than *Rain Man*, and a lot more honest." "De Niro goes places Hoffman never dreamed of going." "It's a hit, and if it wins Best Picture, straight through the roof."

The Bonfire of the Vanities (Warner Bros.). "The absolute stinker of the season." "Every decision they could have made they made wrong." "I hear they're trying to turn it into a comedy now, which is an okay idea, I guess, except I also hear nobody's laughing." "Here's the deal. It cost over 60 and it's testing badly, but people are going to go. At least at the start. Too much hype to ignore. This is not *Ishtar* by any means. What's sad is it's a waste of money and time and talent and material."

Havana (Universal). The most controversial in this category. "I heard long and terrific." "I heard long and dull." "Redford looked great." "Redford looked bad." "I thought Redford looked bad, but my wife thought Redford looked great." "It doesn't matter about a picture like this, and I'll tell you why. It's like *Dick Tracy*. The studio will spend so much money advertising it, the public will have to go. It will do a hundred million dollars, I promise you—but I'm not saying it will make money, which is the craziness of the business we're in."

The Russia House (MGM-Pathe). "This is *Mermaids* all

over again. A quality film that will get crushed by the competition. Should have been moved. I know that. I also knew *Dead Poets Society* would be a disaster."

The Sheltering Sky (Warner Bros.). "Bertolucci's first since *The Last Emperor*. So there will be a lot of interest. But it's already started opening in Europe to mixed reviews and worse business. Not this time." So said one, so said them all.

FINAL THOUGHTS

The movie that most people wanted to talk about was not a holiday opening: *Dances With Wolves*. That was the one on their minds. And they *loved* it. "A lock for the nominations." "Just a triumph for Costner. And you know what I heard? He didn't enjoy the experience all that much, would rather act. Maybe won't ever direct again. Would *that* be a waste."

Misery (Columbia). I've saved this for last because, as the screenwriter, I know the most about it. Rob Reiner thinks it's his best work. Stephen King is wild about it, and he doesn't remotely care for what's been done with his books. I've seen the movie absolutely thrill preview audiences. James Caan, out to pasture a year ago, is already flooded with multi-million-dollar offers. Kathy Bates is a wonder. The test results have already been in the L.A. press, and they are startling.

So will it do a hundred million?

Answer No. 1: "It won't, but it might have, except this is the worst time of the year to bring it out. A Stephen King movie? Even a good one. At Christmas? Dumb." Answer No. 2: "It will fly right past it, and you know why? Because it's coming out at the perfect time. No competition for this kind of picture. The whole field to yourselves. Christmas. Brilliant."

We'll reconvene in late January. By then, the truths will have been told. But remember: Only four have a shot. Four at the most. Four out of *Godfather* and *Talking Too* and *Predator 2* and *Down Under* and *Rocky V* and *Little Lady* and *Scissorhands* and *Green Card* and *Home Alone* and *Kindergarten Cop* and *Mermaids* and *Alice* and *Awakenings* and *Havana* and *Russia House* and *Dances With Wolves* and *Misery*.

Over to you.

—NOVEMBER 26, 1990

They Lost It at the Movies

A Reel-To-Reel Recap

Let me start with what people in television call "a grabber." Here it is: This past holiday period was the most important month in fifteen years and one of the two most important in modern movie history.

Now that—in theory—I've got your attention, let me backtrack. This—the last of three articles about holiday films—had its genesis eight or nine months ago when someone read me a list of movies due to come out between Thanksgiving and Christmas this past year. My initial instinct was that they had gone crazy Out There. Too many expensive pictures in much too small a window. Things had to change.

I was right and I was wrong. Things did change. More movies were added.

I interviewed any number of West Coast Wise Men— these are really bright people, by the way, and I mean that— about which movies they thought would hit the currently magical number: $100 million at the box-office. Just before the countdown, the cinch trio was *Godfather III*, *Kindergarten Cop*, and *Three Men and a Little Lady*.

So how did the experts do? As one said to me last week, nervously laughing all the while, "I missed everything, didn't I? Everything. I didn't get anything right. Did anybody get anything right?"

Nope.

Before we start, a word about "the numbers," which is often what they say when they mean "money." For two reasons, many of the figures that follow are simply guesses. (1) If I say a movie cost $25 million, they might reply, "Is that 'hard'?" Meaning, is that the cost of actually making the movie itself (which is what "hard" means), or does it include stuff like studio overhead (10 to 25 percent), loan interest, and such? (2) The truth often becomes a foreign object in the studios' mouths when the subject of costs arises, because it really is their private business. Plus, for no logical reason, some movies get pasted for their budgets (*Ishtar, Heaven's Gate, Legal Eagles*) while others escape (*Die Hard 2*, for example, cost more to make than any of these three).

My arbitrary categories are "Hits," "Disappointments," "flops," and "Disasters." But first, off in a world of wonder, "*Home Alone.*"

HOME ALONE

The making of *Star Wars* was agony. The movie was over budget. Young George Lucas was directing his first "big" film. The lunatic special effects seemed to take forever to shoot. The locations were miserable. A total wipeout in the making.

I have a friend who worked on the picture, and he told me that there was one beacon in the murk. (I believe, but I'm not sure, that it was the locations manager.) While everyone else was slipping toward panic, this guy kept shouting, "You're all mad, don't you see? This is going to be the most successful movie of all time."

In my research, there was no such figure on *Home Alone*. People thought it might do well, maybe a "double," as they sometimes refer to pictures that take in a splendid $50 million.

But one of the biggest pictures of all time? (Some people predict it may actually end up third, behind *E.T.* and *Star Wars*,) Now pundits are telling us why. "You see, it's every child's fantasy," they say. Or "It's so obvious—it's the dream of the child in all of us."

Total bulls—.

No one knows remotely why. It's John Hughes at his best. It can't hurt Rupert Murdoch. At the least, it added a new verb to Hollywoodese: "to be *Home Alone*d." More than one executive said to me, "My picture did 40, but it would have done 50 if we hadn't been *Home Alone*d."

HITS

I'm leaving out *Dances With Wolves*, Kevin Costner's triumph, because it opened too soon to be included but is a huge success. And final word isn't in yet on *Alice*, which looks to be a disappointment.

Awakenings. As with several other films, the results will depend not just on word of mouth but on Oscar.

Edward Scissorhands. Tim Burton is now a major force, in a commercial class with Ivan Reitman and Steven Spielberg and Bob Zemeckis.

Green Card and *Mermaids.* I'm listing them together because several felt they were the same movie—charming comedies with talented people.

Kindergarten Cop. Definitely *Home Alone*d. Did well, eventually maybe 85 at the box-office, but it would have gone over 100 if John Hughes had stayed home. Schwarzenegger is now one of the two biggest stars in the world, along with Tom Cruise. (More on stars later.)

Misery. A solid double. And if you didn't like Kathy Bates, I'm going to pick up all my marbles and go home. (I'm biased. I wrote the screenplay.)

DISAPPOINTMENTS

The Godfather Part III. Fabulous opening and then the slide. No one knows the exact cost. The lowest estimate I heard, from a biased source, was 55 million. The highest, from an equally biased source, was well over 80.

The truth probably lies in between, which would mean—if you throw in all the additional money spent on prints, advertising, etc.—that we might be talking about the first $100-million American movie.

Look Who's Talking Too. "They ruined a franchise. They rushed it out. It needed reshooting, and everyone knew that."

The Rescuers Down Under. "Lovely to look at. And who cared?" Crushed by *Home Alone*.

Three Men and a Little Lady. Just before it opened, the opinion was that it'd be a cinch 150 million, maybe 200. Then I heard, "Huge, 120 easy." Then it was "at least 90." Probably it will end up in the high sixties. Expectations were devastated. The most *Home Alone*d of all.

FLOPS

Come See the Paradise. Several of my correspondents argued that it should be listed under "Disasters." But for me, disaster implies a fall, and no one expected anything out of this baby.

Predator 2. There will be no *Predator 3*.

Rocky V. Many argued that this should be under "Disappointments." But what carried the day was how the audience for the character had shriveled. "It goes so fast out here. Here he is, the star of the eighties, and suddenly Rambo is gone and Rocky is gone. He's doing comedy now, but the last attempt at that was *Rhinestone*. I wouldn't want to be his agent. That's a lie—I would kill to be his agent. But what I really would like is to *have been* his agent. Then I'd retire and get out of this madness."

The Rookie. "I hate to say this, but Clint [Eastwood] is in trouble. Here's a flick that should appeal to his people, where he's coupled with a young guy [Charlie Sheen] to bring in the kids, and . . . down the tubes. He's been the most consistent star since forever, but it's getting shaky, and I hate to see that."

The Russia House. "Except for the leads' acting, what was that? Why was it a movie anyway?"

The Sheltering Sky. Easily the second most disliked movie of the season. (You can probably guess what they hated the most. You're right.)

DISASTERS

Almost an Angel. "I could tell from the preview that it wasn't *It's a Wonderful Life*, but Jesus, no one went. The *'Crocodile' Dundee*s were amazing successes. This must have lost 25 million. And I'm being kind."

Alphabetically now, the Big Two: *Bonfire of the Vanities* and *Havana*.

"What can I say about them? I think it's safe to predict they won't be remembered as overlooked masterpieces. I'll tell you what I'm pretty sure of: No two giant disasters have ever opened so close together." The consensus was that they would lose a total of $100 million.

The feelings aroused by the two movies were totally different. *Havana* was summed up like this: "Too long, too long. Robert Redford was terrific, but he stayed away too long. It was not in any way a bad picture. It was just talky and dull."

I've never heard the kind of hatred that *Bonfire* evoked. "The stench will last for years." "I'd heard about it, so I didn't go to see the movie as much as view the corpse." "There was only one good thing about it. Guber and Peters are famous for shacking up with movies that their names are on but that they had zero to do with, like *Rain Man*. It was fun watching them distance themselves from *Bonfire*."

So why was this Christmas important? Because two things happened that have to change the industry:

(1) Sequels died.

(2) Stars didn't deliver.

The most important month in decades was June 1975,

when *Jaws* opened. No film had ever made so much so quickly, and two fads were born: the decision to make mainly block-busters and the special effects craze. (I know of one studio head who turned down a project, saying, "I don't think it could make more than a million dollars, and I'm not in business to make a million dollars.")

That madness became endemic.

Sequels poisoned the air, and everyone was happy be-cause they were easy to advertise and people wanted them.

Forget it.

Stars got really obscene salaries. Five million is what you paid for someone you *didn't* want.

Forget it.

At least that's what I say.

"Next Christmas will be absolutely different," one exec-utive told me. "Absolutely different and exactly the same. Next year, we won't make this year's mistakes; we'll make next year's mistakes." "The reason the business won't change," a top agent said, "is very simple: It's the Big Dick syndrome. All the studio heads have to posture—they can't retreat from the battlefield."

Some thought there would be change. "Sure, some. But stars are what Hollywood has always been about, and they add a certain cachet for the foreign market."

Personally, I think 1991 will be more of the garbage we've had this year. (I can't make a ten-best list. I can't even make a five-best list with any conviction.) Movies take a long time to make, and 1991 is already in the pipeline.

But after that, only the Shadow knows.

All I'm sure of is this: They're scared Out There. This Christmas, while Hollywood was apres-skiing in Aspen, the Earth moved.

—FEBRUARY 18, 1991

Capos and Indians

Oscar '91: Italians vs. Stallions

"I don't want to talk about the Oscars," a studio executive said. "It's so horrible. You people back East don't understand something—we don't just *make* pictures, we have to go out and *see* them. And this year has been, all in all, putting as happy a face on it as I can, this year has been—well, does 'stomach-turning' sum it up?"

In truth, none of the people I interviewed were enthusiastic about the 1990 output. The highest rating anyone gave it was "maybe fair." One fellow assured me it was "the worst in memory, and I am very old."

What stunned them was the generally low level of what was out there. "I felt really rotten about the industry," one top executive said. "The people came. Commercially, it was terrific. But my God, if we keep giving them what we gave them, when does the spigot turn off?"

And so we slink to this year's Oscars.

What follows is the opinion of the opinionmakers on four major categories: Best Actor, Best Actress, Best Director, and Best Picture. No matter how much their thoughts varied, all the people interviewed were alike in one respect: They had no passion whatsoever.

BEST ACTOR

- Kevin Costner, *Dances With Wolves*

- Robert De Niro, *Awakenings*

- Gerard Depardieu, *Cyrano de Bergerac*

- Richard Harris, *The Field*

- Jeremy Irons, *Reversal of Fortune*

Kevin Costner: "I think his only chance is if it's a sweep. He would be the beneficiary. But he would be the caboose of a sweep, not the engine."

Robert De Niro: "Everything tells me yes, except I think no. Mainly because he's won before with better work and he'll do better work again. Plus this: It's all expectation out here. The expectation had *Awakenings* as the movie of the year. And then it didn't perform. It disappointed the Academy. At least, that's my guess."

Gerard Depardieu: "He's a great actor, no question, but the only foreign language winner, I think, was Sophia Loren, and didn't she have some kind of hardship that year? Like when Elizabeth Taylor won for *Butterfield 8*. It was really an Oscar for survival. If Depardieu had been sick this year, he might have had an outside shot. Seriously ill, he might even have been a front-runner. But no way when he's healthy."

Richard Harris: "He should win—not for his performance in the picture but for his performance in getting nominated. He was magic. He worked the town better than Reagan ever worked a room. There wasn't a voter's cheek he didn't kiss."

Jeremy Irons: "I think he's going to win, and I'll tell you why: super performance. But that's not it. The picture didn't do business, *but it wasn't expected to*. It's sort of the reverse of De Niro in *Awakenings*. And it was a classy film. The Academy likes to be associated with class."

Consensus: The winner will be Anthony Hopkins for *The Silence of the Lambs*. Oops, sorry, not eligible. But more than one of my correspondents felt that if *Lambs* had opened for one week in L.A., thereby making it eligible for this year, Hopkins would have breezed home. (They also felt that he would not win next year because people tend to forget movies that open early.)

For this year, then, Costner if *Dances With Wolves* sweeps. Otherwise, Irons.

BEST ACTRESS

- Kathy Bates, *Misery*
- Anjelica Huston, *The Grifters*
- Julia Roberts, *Pretty Woman*
- Meryl Streep, *Postcards From the Edge*
- Joanne Woodward: *Mr. and Mrs. Bridge*

Kathy Bates: She is a lock to win, because "it's the duckling turning into a swan. She came out of nowhere and was wonderful. And the Academy goes for that."

She has no chance whatsoever to win, because "*Misery* is not what the Academy honors. It's a horror film. They didn't give it to Bette Davis, and they'll never give it to Kathy Bates."

Anjelica Huston: She is a lock to win, because "the critics couldn't stop raving. If she doesn't win, that means the Academy lines up with the Philistines."

She has no chance whatsoever to win, because "everybody out here hated the movie. And I don't think they're dying to take Huston to lunch, either. Which might be the nicest thing anybody ever needs to have said about them."

Julia Roberts: She is a lock to win, because "Hollywood has fallen in love with her like no woman in *decades*. Plus, she's in a big hit now—*Sleeping With the Enemy*—and that affects voters."

She has no chance whatsoever to win, because "we have to maintain *some* standards out here. An Oscar for a movie like *Pretty Woman*—get hold of yourself."

Meryl Streep: She is a lock to win, because "there's no logical competition. The picture did a little business. She sang some. And Hollywood's got this fixation on her talent."

She has no chance whatsoever to win, because "the town is cooling on her. Anyway, she was miscast—too old. And besides, I couldn't stand it if she won again."

Joanne Woodward: She is a lock to win, because "she was wonderful, and it's the kind of movie that wins awards. It's an artsy film, and not many of those get nominated, but if they do, they tend to do well."

She has no chance whatsoever to win, because "she's won already [*The Three Faces of Eve*]. But that's not it. She *hates* Hollywood. That's not criticism—*I* hate Hollywood, and I *live* here. But she lives in Connecticut, has no interest in the town. Inconceivable the Academy will give it to her."

Consensus: There isn't going to be a Best Actress winner this year.

BEST DIRECTOR AND PICTURE

Best Director Nominees

• Francis Ford Coppola, *The Godfather, Part III*

• Stephen Frears, *The Grifters*

• Barbet Schroeder, *Reversal of Fortune*

Best Picture Nominees

• *Awakenings*

• *Ghost*

• *The Godfather Part III*

If you are confused because you thought there were supposed to be five nominees in each category, a basic truth needs explaining. As one agent put it, "You know how they always list the ten movies that did the most business over the weekend? Fine. But don't interpret that to mean that *any* of them are doing much business—they are just doing more business than those below."

And the names and movies above? "There have to be five nominees. But this year, only two have any chance. The others are strictly salad." Saying good-bye to the salad above, then, what follows are the front-runners. "If both of them lose, it will be Dewey-Truman all over again, squared."

Best Director *and* Picture Nominees

- Kevin Costner, *Dances With Wolves*
- Martin Scorsese, *GoodFellas*

Unanimous sentiment that these were the two outstanding films of the year. No one even had a picture to put third. And except for the talent level involved, they couldn't be much more different.

Martin Scorsese directed fifteen films before *GoodFellas*. His most famous, more than likely, are *Taxi Driver* and *Raging Bull*. The latter is considered the best film of the eighties and won Scorsese his first nomination as a director. (He was honored again for *The Last Temptation of Christ*.) He has never won.

But the feeling about him is this: He may be the finest working director in America. He has also never had a breakthrough hit. And perhaps because of that, right now he is on a remarkable roll. "Do you know why the critics slobbered over *The Grifters*?" one star told me. "It sure wasn't the picture. Don't laugh. I think it was Scorsese's name attached as producer." In other words, this is an underappreciated major talent who is cresting at the perfect time.

Kevin Costner had never directed before he did *Dances With Wolves*. And with the success of the film, all the supposed mistakes have been forgiven and forgotten, although Costner probably remembers the abuse and the joking. The movie was forever being referred to as "Kevingate."

The fact that he is inexperienced and an actor does not work against him. Robert Redford won for *Ordinary People*, Warren Beatty for his first solo effort, *Reds*.

In other words, this is a no-longer-underappreciated major talent who is, at the moment, *the* Golden Boy.

But this year, there is an unusual element, and it's this: geography.

Scorsese isn't just a guy out of Flushing, Queens. He's NYU film school. And the majority of his movies have New York as their locale.

And they *feel* New York. *GoodFellas* is "sharp," "urban," "tough and bloody." "It's an absolutely in-your-face movie."

Costner, a Californian, produced a grand epic—romantic, even operatic at times—dealing with the West.

"I'll tell you what I think," an executive explained. "If you guys were voting, if the whole nine-hour Oscar show was done at Radio City, I think *GoodFellas* would win. I'm assuming, obviously, that the bulk of the voting would take place back East. But it doesn't, and *GoodFellas* won't."

Another opinion: "*GoodFellas* was just brilliantly crafted. I don't know a director who didn't get blown away by it. But the gore. All that blood. The Academy is sincere, but they're also old and they live here. *Dances* dances away with it. Will you use that line? I don't get much cleverer. '*Dances* dances away.' Actually, I read it someplace."

One final bit of wisdom, this from a studio head: "You

don't comprehend the effect *Dances* has had out here. It broke every conceivable Hollywood rule. It defied all the wisdom of our daily lives. When a picture like that explodes—and they're rare, believe me—they do something to us: All our notions have to be reconceived. Forget the success of the flick or the problems Costner had or his achievement We're all thinking differently now. About Westerns. About subtitles. About the length a picture can be. About movies with quills."

Consensus: Costner and Costner, over and out.

—MARCH 25, 1991

THE FOLLOWING WERE ACADEMY AWARD WINNERS FOR 1990:

Best Actor	*Jeremy Irons, Reversal of Fortune*
Best Actress	*Kathy Bates,Misery*
Best Picture	*Dances with Wolves*
Best Director	*Kevin Costner, Dances with Wolves*

Tears and Fears

Hollywood Hunkers Down

What with the fall of communism, there's only one concern of genuine intellectual weight remaining: How *is* Hollywood doing?

A couple of facts are undeniable. These past months, three pictures flashed into blockbuster status, having taken in the requisite $100 million at the box-office, helping to make this the third-highest-grossing summer in history. With that in mind, the answer should not surprise anyone: Right now, as memories of sweet corn recede, the feeling of gloom Out There goes deeper than it has in years. And it is growing by the day.

I'll try to make sense of that eventually, but other seasonal items must be dealt with first: The fall of the million-dollar screenwriter. The rise of the black film director. And, of course, stars—and, more specifically, how they are judged.

TELESCOPING THE STARS

It was once possible to say there were Space Stars and there were Dollar Stars. Space Stars were those you read about in the supermarkets but wouldn't plunk down your money to see. Once Raquel Welch. Now Roseanne Barr. Eastwood was the perfect Dollar Star—low-key, few if any interviews, amazingly popular in theaters around the world.

Today, the Dollar Star has become Hollywood's answer to the complete game in baseball—a quaint, disappearing reminder of the sweet used-to-be.

Now all the stars do publicity. Sometimes it's in their contracts, more often not. Sometimes they are skilled at it, more often not. Almost without exception, they detest it. (So would you.)

No one matches Arnold Schwarzenegger at skillful publicity. He is bright, willing, inexhaustible, conscientious—the best. He is also something we haven't had in a while: not just the biggest star in the world but acknowledged to be that *unanimously*. (Usually, there are at least two vying for the honor. A few years back, the argument was between Sylvester Stallone, Bill Murray, and Eddie Murphy.) One studio executive put it this way: "Arnold's had *four* home runs in a row. *Twins*, *Total Recall*, *Kindergarten Cop*, and now *Terminator 2*. I can't think of the last time anyone did that."

Ranked second, also without question—Kevin Costner. Another Suit explained, "He was just a middle-range star until recently. *Bull Durham*, *Field of Dreams*. Nice pictures, nice successes. Then came a total wipeout, *Revenge*, and he was shaky."

But with two worldwide triumphs—*Dances with Wolves* and *Robin Hood: Prince of Thieves*—*Revenge* is forgotten. "I would do anything legal to get him," the Suit said. "And I'd do anything illegal to get Arnold."

Third place is a three-way tie between Tom Cruise, Mel Gibson and Julia Roberts (billing, of course, is alphabetical). If Roberts's presence surprises you, that may be because you've read about her summer "flop," *Dying Young*. A lot was written about how Roberts might possibly follow her meteoric rise with a suitably meteoric fall.

"I hate reading that garbage," a studio executive said. "We have so much bulls— in our business anyway, I just go crazy when misconceptions are kept alive. Tell your readers this: *How a picture does is not how we judge stars*. There's only the one criterion: Does the picture *open?*"

Movies have become, in other words, a first-weekend business. And stars are paid to generate that business. Then, if the picture is pleasing and grosses a lot, fine. If it goes off a cliff, not so fine but, from the star's point of view, bearable. "We don't hold stars responsible for quality," said the executive. "Or word of mouth. *Dying Young* took in over $9 million that first weekend, and Roberts is still the first bankable female star since Streisand."

SCRIPTS AND SCRIP

We all saw the lists of young writers who caught lightning. We all read the stories about the studio feeding frenzy over acquiring original action screenplays, "spec scripts."

Every executive I interviewed agreed it was a freak phenomenon, and it would never happen again.

I am aware that many of the individuals I interview fib to me on occasion, or rearrange facts. But here I swear to you they are correct. The million-dollar craze is done.

And how do I know this?

The truth shall set us free: because it never happened.

Hollywood has always been aware of the Dutch-tulip-bulb madness. But this was *amazing*. They absolutely believed their own bull—. "I loved it," one top guy admitted about the rumors swirling through town. "We bought a '$2 million' original. Fabulous publicity. Phone rang off the wall."

And the reality?

"You mean dollars? We actually paid 400,000."

A lot of money, true, but still a tad less than 2 million. So how did that number emerge? "This isn't really precise, but the rest was on the come. A producer's fee if the movie happened. All kinds of options, the next first draft—you know, *stuff*. It did add up to 2 million, but one million six was phony."

The feeling is that they were certainly suspect, many of them phony, except for two: Shane Black's *The Last Boy Scout*, which generated "the craze," and Joe Eszterhas's *Basic Instinct*, which topped it out. "I haven't seen the contracts, but I believe those two are legit," one agent explained. Even Willy Loman knew that a couple of sales don't constitute a craze-hell, they're not even an aberration.

Dueling P.R. people, that's what it was.

BLACK IS BEAUTIFUL

Of course, credit must go to Spike Lee, with a healthy nod to Mario Van Peebles.

But what this is really about is John Singleton, who

wrote and directed *Boyz N the Hood*, and who is young, gifted, and black.

"You want to know what's crazy?" one top guy said. "Remember, this is not about talent; it's just how we think out here. But right now, Singleton, off just the one movie, is more important than Spike Lee. I know how that sounds, and I know that Lee is a major, *major* talent. But he is also hard-hitting, political, and issue-oriented. Of course, the Singleton was *about* something, but what we like about it—it was so damn entertaining. *People went to see it.*"

And the interest in black directors?

"You won't believe this, but I do. Black is not the issue; box-office is. I don't think, when I hire, Is this guy green or not? I think, Will he *make me* some green or not?"

"This 'rise' business—if it lasts, there's only going to be one reason: The pictures did business. I'll go to my grave on this: Hollywood is not about sex. It's also not about power. We're like any other business: money. I don't think that's so terrible. Show me a business that isn't."

I don't know if that's terrible or not, but for me, sex and power don't even come in second.

Ego does. In a walkover.

THE SUMMER OF '91

"I'm not panicked, I'm gloomy," a famous executive said. "And I'll admit it, the gloom is becoming pervasive. Because, yes, money was made this summer, no question. But look who made it: the independents. Carolco had *Terminator 2*; Morgan Creek had *Robin Hood*; *City Slickers* was Castle Rock's. Those were the big three. And fourth? *Naked Gun 2 1/2*, a sequel. *Backdraft* took fifth—another independent. Now *I'm* running a studio. I've got all this overhead, I've got all these top executives on salary for their wisdom—and we struck out. We struck out, and *I don't know what to do about it.*"

One agent explained, "Remember, summer is dream-come-true time. That's when they release their big-budget no-brainers and the money rolls in. You're allowed to have disappointments in the fall. My God, you *expect* disappointments in February. But summer is for sure shots. And this summer, they weren't there.

"If a major studio had one of the big pictures, they could have used it as a hedge against disasters—*Terminator 2* might have paid for *Hudson Hawk*. There was no protection this time."

Back to the studio head: "I can explain my gloom. Three reasons. First, the fall looks dreadful. Second, the recession hit us in a way we didn't expect: The big pictures were still big, but it used to be impossible to spend 10 million advertising a new movie and open it in 1,500 theaters and have no one come. Tell that to the guys who had *Return to the Blue Lagoon.*

"But the third reason is crucial: For years, we've known that the cost of making movies has been skyrocketing. And the money we've been taking in has been sort of flat. But the revenue line was *always* greater than the cost line. Well, this summer, *those graphs crossed.* For the first time in my memory, at least right now, movies are a loss business . . . . "

Can costs come down? "Mine will," another executive told me. "Believe that."

I don't, and here's why. One of his new productions has a veteran action star in the lead. This was a movie with many locations. And the star wanted a thousand a night for a hotel room. Not unusual. Plus $3,000 a week cash in spending money. Yawn—on to the next. Well, the next concerned his entourage. Here's what the star demanded:

1) a stand-in

2) a double

3) a trainer

4) an assistant

5) a driver

6) a cook

7) someone to handle wardrobe

8) someone to handle makeup

9) someone to handle hair

10) and—pay attention, please—his personal *hair colorist.*

All ten to go first class, to traipse after him everywhere.

Guess who folded?

The gloomy studio head was speaking again. "I feel better because I just remembered something. When I said the fall was going to be bad? That was silly of me—sometimes we get caught up in our own gossip. Our world is not like yours, and we have to remember this: *Dances With Wolves* was the worst picture ever made—until people saw it."

—SEPTEMBER 16, 1991

DREAMING OF A TIGHT CHRISTMAS

HOLLYWOOD'S HEAVY HOLIDAY HEART

The current mood out there can be summed up with one question: Is this merely the worst panic in 10 years or the worst in 25?

A little perspective. The holiday season a decade past had a grand total of one (count it, one) breakaway hit—*On Golden Pond*—and ten wipeouts. Grown men still tremble when they talk about it. But their elders shiver when they remember the late sixties, which had the studios scrambling to pay the Burtons a million each to star in stuff like *Boom!* (exclamation point theirs). The reason for this panic is simple. Costs are murderous and rocketing; revenues are flat. And the studios feel helpless to stop the bleeding. "I don't know what the hell people want," one executive said. "Look at *Frankie and Johnny*. Pacino, *Sea of Love*. Garry Marshall from *Pretty Woman*. Pfeiffer. A terrific play. Laughs, sex, romance—*everything the audience wants*. *Huge* disappointment." He paused. "People aren't going to anything now." A longer pause. "They just better come at Christmas, that's all . . . . "

What will we be standing in line for this holiday season? Or (and this is the Nightmare) will we give the movies a pass?

What follows is not intended to be a complete list. And we are not talking quality. The subject under discussion is really this: vulnerability. Dede Allen, the great film editor, once said, "Every movie has a soft underbelly."

And that is how we're going to look at what's coming. Strengths and weaknesses. The following opinions came from Hollywood's Powers. They had seen none of the films. This is their reality.

SEQUELS

An American Tail: Fievel Goes West (Universal).

Strengths: "It's a sequel." "Not that many kid films."

Underbelly: "It's a sequel." "*Rescuers Down Under* didn't do it."

Star Trek VI (Paramount).

Strengths: "Those lunatic fans that first weekend."

Underbelly: "What if it's even worse than *Star Trek V*?"

ALL BUT THE BIG TWO

The Addams Family (Paramount—Raul Julia, Anjelica Huston).

Strengths: "Recognizability." "Good ad campaign—they're making you believe you're going to have a lot of fun." "I'll shock you—it will not dumb out the audience."

Underbelly: "Is it any good? The buzz is mixed." "Anybody who tells you it's good is lying."

Beauty and the Beast (Disney).

Strengths: "If it's what Disney says, no weaknesses." "The No. 2 flick of the season."

Underbelly: "Disney can screw up anything."

Bugsy (TriStar—Warren Beatty, Annette Bening).

Strengths: "Barry Levinson." "Warren got her pregnant at the perfect time."

Underbelly: "Who wants gangster pictures? Especially at Christmas." "Does anybody want to see Beatty miscast?"

Cape Fear (Universal—Robert De Niro, Nick Nolte, Jessica Lange).

Strengths: "Really talented people doing what they do best." "Scorsese is a darling now—the audience thinks *GoodFellas* was his first film."

Underbelly: "Violent." "Tough, graphic." "I hear it's really good, but no one says it's what you'd call 'fun.' "

Father of the Bride (Disney—Steve Martin, Diane Keaton, Martin Short).

Strengths: "Only straight-on comedy this Christmas." "Steve Martin is always good in a comedy."

Underbelly: "Will they think they've seen it already on TV? "Disney marketing."

For the Boys (Twentieth Century Fox—Bette Midler, James Caan). *Strengths*: "I hear it's good." "Midler in a musical."

Underbelly: "Midler's not a star unless she's funny, and this is a drama." "Why will kids care about USO entertainers?"

Grand Canyon (Twentieth Century Fox—Kevin Kline,

Steve Martin, Mary McDonnell, Danny Glover).

Strengths: "Larry Kasdan directing." "*Big Chill II*, sort of." "Very good word."

Underbelly: "What happened to the Big Chill generation isn't nice to contemplate." "Rotten trailer." "It's not flashy, and Christmas needs some hubbub."

JFK (Warner Bros.—Kevin Costner, Sissy Spacek, Gary Oldman, Donald Sutherland).

Strengths: "Kevin Costner." "Oliver Stone's passion." "Don't believe what you hear about Costner's accent—if he can survive Nottingham, he'll get by New Orleans."

Underbelly: "Are we bored with the subject?" "Three hours long?" "Either huge or a flop."

The Last Boy Scout (Warner Bros.—Bruce Willis, Damon Wayans—and a script by Shane Black that sold for more than $1 million).

Strengths: "I liked the screenplay, but . . . zero. *Zero*, do you hear me?" "None. Believe me, not a strength in sight."

Underbelly: "How do they hide Bruce Willis's name in this one?" "All those prehistoric elements we all hoped had gone away." "Willis and Joel Silver really think the audience is full of dolts and morons."

My Girl (Columbia—Macaulay Culkin, Dan Aykroyd, Jamie Lee Curtis).

Strengths: "Macaulay Culkin."

Underbelly: "Macaulay Culkin dies."

Prince of Tides (Columbia—Nick Nolte, Barbra Streisand).

Strengths and *Underbelly*: "Streisand. I think she's fabulous, and

I hope it works. Because of who she is and what she's accomplished, there will be intense focus on the picture. I liked the book. It was deeply emotional. But it wasn't a vehicle. If she turns it into a picture about her, if it's another *Yentl*—death. In other words, her ego is the underbelly."

Three movies are being released in limited runs in hopes of getting Oscar nominations: *At Play in the Fields of the Lord, Fried Green Tomatoes*, and *Rush*. "I hear some good stuff, but if they don't catch lightning like *Driving Miss Daisy*," said one Power, "blink and they'll be gone."

THE BIG TWO

Hook (TriStar—Robin Williams, Julia Roberts, Dustin Hoffman, Bob Hoskins).

Strengths: "Everything. Spielberg doing the kind of things he understands. Dustin, Robin, Julia. Not to mention Hoskins and Maggie Smith, who just might be the greatest actress in the world. No stone unturned." "They will spend a fortune in hyping. I heard the cost was 81 million hard, and 40 percent of the gross: That works out to close to 125 million. The most expensive movie of all time."

Underbelly: "*You* find one. The picture of the season." "Absolutely the top picture of the season." So say several more. But not all. "I heard it was a great script. Then I heard they couldn't stop rewriting it." "Peter Pan is about *not* growing up. Why is Peter Pan the adult such a great idea?" "Peter Pan is about whimsy, and whimsy is fragile, and the production could bloat the heart." "I hope it's a hit. My job is shaky if it isn't a hit. Hell, the *industry* is shaky if it isn't a hit. We're talking about the biggest picture since—dare I say it?—*Bonfire of the Vanities*."

Most important of all: *All I Want for Christmas* (Paramount—Thorn Birch, Ethan Randall). No, that is not a joke. And yes, it isn't even a holiday picture. It is Brandon Tartikoff's first Paramount effort. Not that important yet. But if you check *Variety*, you see that the big baseball picture *A League of Their Own*, with Tom Hanks, Geena Davis, and Madonna started shooting on July 10. And is scheduled to come out *next* summer.

Well, *All I Want for Christmas* started shooting twelve days *later*. And opened November 8. *Last* November 8.

"You want to know what Tartikoff's done? He's made the first television movie that will open wide. If it's a hit, it changes maybe everything."

Tartikoff's gambling that there's a window for a kid's picture. And postproduction, which many film people feel is the most important time in the making of a movie, was essentially made invisible.

"He brought it in for nothing. Under 15 million, I heard. And they had a test—I really think this is true—they had a test screening, a test-market screening—are you hearing me?—these grown-up guys had a test-market screening for—listen to me—for *500 six-year-olds*."

A FEW PERSONAL NOTES

• I started in the picture business in '64, so the panic of a few years later didn't mean much to me. But I remember ten years ago, and this is worse.

• Understand: The movie business, because it deals entirely in fantasy, is more prone than most others to this: perception. The impeccable A. D. Murphy of *Variety* estimates that 1991 will be the third-biggest-grossing year ever.

So is the panic logical?

No. But when was Hollywood?

If Christmas works, they'll think their industry is strong and that they are loved, and the spring will be back in their step.

• I've read the Larry and Meg Kasdan screenplay for *Grand Canyon*, and it's the best, for me, in years. The advance word on the movie is strong. If it flops, and if the other quality holiday efforts go down the tubes—and there may well be a lot of quality movies this season—it's on our heads. And look out. As in so many other things, we get the movies we deserve . . . .

Assuming there is a Hollywood, we'll talk about it next year.

—NOVEMBER 18, 1991

PUSHING THE ENVELOPE

OSCAR '92: BASIC INSTINCTS

Last year, when *Dances With Wolves* won everything, it seemed fated, unsurprising. Not true. If you had inquired of Hollywood's Powers That Be six weeks sooner, before the nominations came out, you would have found that it was a neck-and-neck race between the Western and *GoodFellas*.

Sometime in those intervening days, a surge began, a trend was established—a shift in voters' perception.

Therefore, this year, I came up with one of the most genuinely dazzling notions in modern cinema history: track the trend. Ferret it out. Zero in on just what did change the minds of those who voted in the four major categories: Best Picture, Best Director, Best Actress, Best Actor.

And so, this year, my informants talked to me twice—once before the nominations, again afterward—so that I might impart to you something no one had ever done before: the actual workings of the Hollywood mind.

Well, my idea turned out to be a total wrap. I would put it only slightly west of the Edsel.

And why?

Come along.

BEST PICTURE

- *Beauty and the Beast*

- *Bugsy*

- *JFK*

- *The Prince of Tides*

- *The Silence of the Lambs*

There are absolutely no surprises here. In the early interviews, all my informants had three locks: *Bugsy, JFK,* and *The Silence of the Lambs.*

"But listen to me, now," one Honcho said. "I'm sure these will be nominated, but I don't think any of them will win."

Why?

"Because," said a peer, "look at them. They all have tremendous strengths and equally enormous forces ranged against them.

"*Bugsy* you could track back to *Bonnie and Clyde.* Wonderful, skillful work. But does the academy want to honor an insane killer who, after all, did not break ground for the Sistine Chapel? I don't think he invented Vegas. It was humming right along. What Siegel did do was put a hotel on the Strip. That we're gonna honor?

"*JFK* is obvious. Great, great technical achievement,

but when did a film of this level of controversy win?

"And *Silence?* A dazzling film about a nut who *eats people?* Remember the age of the Academy."

A third said this back then: "A lot of people think the Oscars should send a positive message to the world. And when there are no leaders, listen to me: *Strange things happen.*"

And my neat notion of a trend?

Zip. "People are so confused right now that no one even wants to predict, because they're afraid they'll come out looking stupid. *The Prince of Tides* could win, helped by a sympathy vote for Barbra's not getting a Director nomination. But a lot of people also thought it was a flawed picture."

Beauty and the Beast?

The sleeper. Although some said it did wonderfully just being the first animated film to get a Best Picture nomination, others hedged. "I just feel it," one lady said. "It was the one to profit most from the nominations. Plus this: People *like* it. And in a crazy year like this one, that could be enough."

BEST DIRECTOR

- Jonathan Demme, *The Silence of the Lambs*
- Barry Levinson, *Bugsy*
- Ridley Scott, *Thelma and Louise*
- John Singleton, *Boyz N the Hood*
- Oliver Stone, *JFK*

Again, weeks ago, three locks: Levinson, Stone, and Demme. And three outside shots: Singleton, Scott, and Streisand.

And again today, no trend whatsoever.

"I don't think either Singleton or Scott is in it," one studio head said. "I'm going to vote for Demme, but he's not going to win. He's not one of us. He doesn't play the game. When he visits, it's like he's on a budget. 'Well I can cut this out or go light on that.' Brilliant director, overdue. Should win. Won't."

"I'll tell you why Oliver Stone won't win," another executive said. "Not just because he's already won twice. It's because he won't shut up. He's making like a political candidate, and we've got enough of them this year."

"Want a theory?" a fellow director said. "*Bugsy* is a movie made for us. People didn't like it. I think it may even end up losing money. And I don't think it's going to win Picture or Actor or most of the others. But I think Barry's going to win. I don't think this has ever happened before, but the Best Director award is going to be a consolation prize."

BEST ACTRESS

- Geena Davis, *Thelma & Louise*

- Laura Dern, *Rambling Rose*

- Jodie Foster, *The Silence of the Lambs*

- Bette Midler, *For the Boys*

- Susan Sarandon, *Thelma & Louise*

Six weeks ago, the top three were Davis, Foster, and Sarandon, with Streisand, Annette Bening (*Bugsy*), Midler, and Kathy Bates (*Fried Green Tomatoes*) as contenders.

Sob—no trends.

"I'm going nutty on this one," an actor told me. "Jodie Foster just won. But she's the new Streep—you can't go wrong voting for her. Davis and Sarandon are going to split the vote. Laura Dern is young; not enough people saw the picture. And Midler only wins if you give an award for heartbreak. She was just crushed, and she didn't hide it. They like that out here."

"It will definitely not be Midler," said an executive. "The movie lost enough to sink a Central American country."

"I think Geena Davis," said another executive. "Yes, I know she just won for *Accidental Tourist*, but that was Supporting. People like her. And this year, that could matter."

"Let me tell you something, Goldman. This was a rotten idea of yours. Don't you understand? You picked a year in which everyone is walking around just as confused as losing horseplayers. There are no sudden ground swells. It's going to be a mystifying evening. If I were you, I'd can your article this year." He doesn't know me that well: I'm all heart.

BEST ACTOR

- Warren Beatty, *Bugsy*

- Robert De Niro, *Cape Fear*

- Anthony Hopkins, *The Silence of the Lambs*

- Nick Nolte, *The Prince of Tides*

- Robin Williams, *The Fisher King*

Trumpets, please. At last—a *trend*.

In the early tallies, two were far ahead: Nolte and Hopkins. Now?

"Over. Shut. Nolte."

"A lock. Nick."

"Not even close."

"Nolte with no one in second."

So what happened?

1) "He's been good a lot, and he's never been recognized."

2) "He's had a lot of personal turmoil, and he's survived."

3) "He's wonderful in the movie."

4) "*Cape Fear* and *Tides* makes a double whammy."

5) "Hollywood loves a comeback story."

6) "People like him—and now they can say he's a star."

7) "I think he's going to win, because he was terrific and because Streisand didn't get nominated for director. It works in his favor. 'See?' people can say, 'she *was* robbed, after all. She got that performance out of him, and then they screwed her. And it'll be great television, the speech he's going to give thanking her.' "

And why did Hopkins disappear?

1) "The picture came out when, February? If it was a holiday flick, it might have been different." (Last year's column on this subject said much the same thing: People tend to forget

movies that open early.)

2) There was a certain wisdom circulating that Hopkins's was more of a supporting role. "I don't know who started that baby," an angry agent (not Hopkins's) said. "You don't judge a part by linage. Impact is what matters. What do you remember of what you saw on the screen? And people for a long time are going to remember Hopkins, just like Tony Perkins in *Psycho*. Which, by the way, didn't win either."

3) "Too tough for the voters, too grisly."

4) "He's British, and usually that's a plus—we all figure anyone who can talk that way has to be smart. But remember, the last two winners were Daniel Day-Lewis [*My Left Foot*] and Jeremy Irons [*Reversal of Fortune*]. Tony's luck just ran out."

"It's going to be the strangest year in memory. Tell your readers not to expect a sweep. Anything could win anything. This may be the first Oscar show in generations that we all watch. I'm kind of curious myself . . . . "

—MARCH 30, 1992

THE FOLLOWING WERE ACADEMY AWARD WINNERS FOR 1991:

Best Picture	*The Silence of the Lambs*
Best Director	*Jonathan Demme, The Silence of the Lambs*
Best Actress	*Jodie Foster, The Silence of the Lambs*
Best Actor	*Anthony Hopkins, The Silence of the Lambs*

DISASTER MOVIES

THE PRICE IS NEVER RIGHT

As I sit here huddled in my parka, woolly mammoths stalk the lawn outside—which means it is Labor Day weekend 1992, and Al Roker is real lucky he's not in my vicinity. I am visiting friends in upstate New York, and I have been forced, out of boredom, to think. Anyone who knows me at all knows we are in serious trouble when that happens.

However, an idea of such breathtaking depth and importance has surfaced that I feel compelled to share it. The Christmas flicks we'll talk about in a couple of months. This is about some movies from the year thus far.

Which has been as pathetic as any in memory. If the Oscar cutoff date were this weekend, *Unforgiven* would sweep everything. (It may well do just that come awards time.) Now, one great movie a year is something we should all settle for. What breaks the heart about these past eight months is that I can recommend only *two* American movies, the other being *One False Move*. (Don't be put off by the violence of the first five minutes.)

I have talked to the usual Powers Out There, and they agree about the awfulness. But not just this year—throw in the past couple as well. "I can't take my kids to anything," one of them said. "It's embarrassing," replied another. Said a third, younger than his peers, "It's all crap, man. C-R-A-P."

This was the first time such admissions had been made to me, and I had to ask if they felt in any way responsible.

"Oh, that's a really smart question, Goldman. I love that question a lot. That's the kind of question that makes me really respect the idiot who asked it" (the youngster speaking).

"Of course I feel responsible. But that's only because I *am*." Pause. "You think it's so easy, you do it."

Why don't you? I asked several.

"I'm chicken. We're all chicken," an Elder answered. "The *cost*. Cost is so brutal, we're all scared of anything remotely original."

Cost. The movie I thought would change their world was *Twins*. It starred Mr. Schwarzenegger and Mr. DeVito, and was whipped into shape by the most successful comedy director of recent times, Mr. Reitman.

They worked for scale. And a gross percentage. The movie was an enormous hit, cost remarkably little, and made everybody richer. It was my naive belief that everyone would start to gamble.

"The agents won't let them," the Elder explained. "The stars are afraid the studios will cheat them, and the agents prey on that. Plus, the agent wants his percentage *now*."

Cost.

No one ever really knows what a movie costs. Everybody lies. Studios are ashamed when something goes out of control, so they lie low. Small pictures try to inflate their importance, so they go the other way.

What follows, then, is not at all accurate. But it may be in the area of the truth, so let's risk it. *Far and Away*, one of the most trumpeted of the summer pictures, starred Tom Cruise and was the kind of film that David Lean, once upon a better time, might have taken an interest in.

Hard cost: $54 million. Stuff: $26 million. Total cost: $80 million. "Hard cost" means the actual money spent to make the movie. "Stuff" means everything else—interest on bank loans, the 1,000 or 2,000 prints, advertising, sending folks hither and yon to hype the project, etc. Total cost can most easily be ascertained by adding hard cost and stuff together.

To date, *Far and Away*'s box-office total in America is in the $50-million range. (This does *not* mean, as so many articles say, that the picture has "earned" $50 million. That's like saying Peter Luger's has "earned" $150 if you and a friend dine there. The studio gets back about half of the box-office take.) *Far and Away* has been described as both a hit and a flop. You decide.

The guess, at the moment, because of the subject matter and Cruise's overseas popularity, is that worldwide box-office might get to $130 million. Meaning approximately $65 million for the studio. Cassette sales, cable-TV sales, regular-TV sales, foreignTV sales, foreign cassettes, and airplanes may well return $20 million more.

So?

You spend 80, you get 85 back.

A hit? Sure.

A flop? Oh, absolutely.

Warren Buffett did not reach his present position in life

by investing $80 million over a couple of years in order to receive $85 million back.

Cost.

We are now venturing toward my Notion. In what follows, I am not referring to movies that do *some* business. I'm interested in two kinds of pictures: giant hits and genuine disasters. Major releases that take in, say, less than $5 million at the box-office, or $100-million-plus.

And my Notion? (And none of the Powers agree with me.) What I think really drives them mad, reinforces their self-admitted fear, is this: In movies of these two types, *quality does not matter*.

Wayne's World could have been dreadfully made. You still would not have been able to keep the public away. *Batman Returns* could have been more inept than *Plan 9 From Outer Space*—there still would have been that stampede. (I know someone who was present at the first sneak of *Star Wars*, fifteen years ago, and swears that when the printed crawl preceding the picture began, the audience broke into applause.)

No one, of course, has the slightest idea when the bottle will trap lightning. (*The Rocketeer* was supposed to blast off.) But I think it's possible to do some after-the-fact quarterbacking if we talk about disasters. In particular, three of recent vintage linger in no one's memory.

Radio Flyer is possibly the costliest unknown disaster in Hollywood history. Some of my experts claim that it lost more than *Havana* or *Hudson Hawk* or *The Bonfire of the Vanities*. No one is saying it wasn't a quality film. A great deal of money was spent on the screenplay. The eventual director, Richard Donner, has done six of the biggest hits of the past years: *The Omen*, *Superman*, *Goonies*, and *Lethal Weapons I, II*, and *III*.

Why did the audience flee? A quick clue: The movie dealt with child abuse.

And who was in it? No stars.

My youngest informant said this: "It's *very* hard, with all the product that keeps opening each Friday, to get the audience's attention if no one's in the picture."

In other words, if *Radio Flyer* had had a star, it would have had a shot.

We've talked about who the stars are before, so I'll make this brief. Arnold on top, closely followed by Costner. Then, on his heels (alphabetically), Cruise, Gibson, and Roberts. All my Powers agree that these are the top five.

But . . . .

What single star most combines quality of performance with box-office power? Think a second. De Niro? Duvall? Hackman? Hoffman? Pacino?

My pick is Jack Nicholson.

Man Trouble was nowhere near the blood-spiller that *Radio Flyer* became. But the feeling Out There is that it will end up losing more than $30 million.

And what was it?

It was a romance.

A romance starring Ellen Barkin.

A romance starring Ellen Barkin and Jack Nicholson.

Explanation? Since he exploded in 1969's *Easy Rider*, Nicholson has made a lot of wonderful films. *Five Easy Pieces* and *Carnal Knowledge* and *Chinatown* and, of course, *Cuckoo's*

Nest and *Terms of Endearment* and *Prizzi's Honor* and *Batman.*

And you know what? He has never, not one time in his 47-picture-and-counting career, starred in a commercially successful *romance.*

The Year of the Comet was by far the least expensive of the three and the one I'm going to talk about in a bit more detail, because I wrote it. it was my first original screenplay after *Butch Cassidy and the Sundance Kid.*

I knew it would be a disaster. How come I'm so smart? Because at the first "sneak," with an audience of perhaps 500, at least 50 left early, never to return. And those who remained let us know they *hated* it.

Being connected with a stiff is an amazing experience. I don't know one single human being not in the movie business who saw it. My own *kids* didn't see it. (My eldest, Jenny, said, "Dad, I meant to, I swear I did, but it disappeared so quickly. I promise I'll catch it on cassette—which I think will be next week.") If any of you happen to rent it, I wouldn't be remotely surprised if your reaction was this: "Hey, that wasn't so bad." And you'd be right. It's an absolutely decent, solidly crafted film.

It's also about vintage wine.

We are at a wine tasting. We're in London; most of the people speak in that loathsome upper-class-lockjaw tone they affect, they use words like *goaty,* and they expectorate what they've sipped into spittoons.

A few minutes later, the crux of the plot becomes clear: The heroine is given the opportunity to catalogue a wine cellar. By this time at that first sneak, the aisles were filled with people stumbling toward the exits. I was seated off in the left corner, each departing creature a knife in the heart.

Now, I love fine red wine. The screenplay exists only because of that passion. But Americans don't, on the whole, care much about wine. And the crucial moviegoing audience, aged 15 to 24, is bored once we move beyond Ripple. All that talk of "bouquet" and "finish" makes it insecure. Maybe if the heroine had been given the job of cataloguing a Lite Beer cellar, we would nave stood a better chance.

Until the exodus at that first sneak, I had no idea what the future of the movie might be. When you're around a film that's forming, you have days when you want to pull the sheets over your head and suck your thumb. You have days when you know you're into the next *Potemkin*. It's a continual swinging torment until the movie is seen by strangers.

Year of the Comet could have opened up a wildly untapped interest in rare wines. Then again, it's also time the public loved Jack in a romance. And child abuse is one of the most talked-about subjects around these days. These movies might have exploded. They didn't.

In 30 years, we'll be able to judge what quality they might have. Never forget that *Singin' in the Rain* was just another Metro tuner when it came out.

For great hits or flops, then, quality is unimportant. So we might as well all just make *Universal Soldier*. That way, no one has to worry.

—SEPTEMBER 28, 1992

A HALLELUJAH CHORUS

HAPPY HOLIDAYS FOR HOLLYWOOD?

Warning: What follows may not be used as a substitute for Desyrel.

Readers of these occasional excursions—which are mostly quotes from the Powers That Be about the State of the Industry—know this to be true: The Powers are at their best when they're wounded. Angry. Jealous. Petty. Filled to the brim with freshly brewed envy.

Not this year. I couldn't find a decent grouse. Because? Because, as impossible as this may be to believe, there are no *Bonfires* lurking out there to singe us. *Hudson Hawk* has flown. (These are the jokes, people.)

The feeling is this: We are about to enter the best seven weeks in years. And not just financially. As one top executive put it, "It's all good. We're gonna be happy."

Granted, this is being written in October, which seems a mite premature to be punditing on films that few have seen. Still, this must be remembered: For Hollywood, Christmas begins this year on November 13, when *Bram Stoker's Dracula* opens.

Usually, these forays spend equal time on both the commercial and the artistic. Because of the perceived brilliance on the horizon, let's get the commercial out of the way quickly.

This feeling was unanimous: there will be three blockbusters, movies that take in more than $100 million at the box-office. Alphabetically, they are:

• *Aladdin*: "It's going to be Disney's biggest animated film yet." "They've locked in on this kind of picture, and they're getting more successful at it all the time."

• *A Few Good Men*: "The complete meal—totally satisfying." "I've seen it, and it's simply unstoppable. Stars, script, direction, plus one more thing: Audiences just love it."

• *Home Alone 2*: "The No. 1 commercial film of the season, if not the year." "We're talking about a force of nature here. It could be twice as bad as the first one, it could be so bad you wouldn't believe it—and it would still go through any roof you might mention."

A lot of other pictures will do well. This from a studio head: "Why do you always glom on to that $100-million number? I think a movie is a hit if it takes in 50 million, and we're going to see a bunch of those."

So say the Wizards. So it must be true. (Caveat: Two years ago, no one had anything remotely enthusiastic to say about the commercial possibilities of *Home Alone*. At least not at this time of year.)

From here on, we are all wearing our artist's hats. What follows, in alphabetical order, is the 1992 holiday selection. (Caveat: Some may drop out; others may be moved up. But as of now, this is what we're looking at.)

• *Aladdin*: "*Beauty and the Beast* got a Best Picture nomination. The only question on this baby is, How does it compare? Some say not quite as fine, some say equal, some say their best yet. But nobody doubts this is one of Disney's major animation efforts."

• *The Bodyguard*: "Kevin Costner in a script by Lawrence Kasdan. How can it be bad?" Another studio head said this: "I think it's going to be good, but I haven't really heard much about it. And I have a rule of thumb: When there's not a lot of news about a major Christmas movie, sometimes that means something. And sometimes what it means isn't so wonderful."

• *Bram Stoker's Dracula* (David Denby's review, page 72): The second most controversial movie of the season. "Francis [Coppola] is incapable of directing a dull film." "I hear it looks incredible, but I also hear it's bloody. You're doing the Dracula story, not *Rebecca of Sunnybrook Farm*, so it's got to be bloody. But I also hear it's an art film. Are those pieces going to mesh?"

• *Chaplin*: One of the three major biographical films coming out at once. I can't remember a similar occurrence since the prime of Mr. Paul Muni. Personal note: I was one of the writer's, so I'll report only what's factual. It has tested extremely well, and Robert Downey Jr., as Charlie Chaplin, has already been touted in several reports as a lock for an Oscar nomination come February 17.

• *The Distinguished Gentleman*: "It's Eddie Murphy back doing what he does best—playing a fish out of water." "I hear good, but I have to add this: It better be. He's been showing contempt for his audience lately, and that's the fastest way I know of being back on television. But if it's another *Trading Places*, it could break out."

• *A Few Good Men*: One comment should suffice, from another studio executive: "I haven't seen it, but a lot of people I know have. I don't have to tell you how competitive this business is—and I have yet to hear one negative *syllable* about it."

• *Forever Young*: It's Mel Gibson, so you know he's going to be good and also that it's going to be around—after all, he's one of the five biggest stars in the world. No. Make that six. Steven Seagal just joined the club, but I'll bet they don't know that yet back in New York." "You know the word I keep hearing about this? *Sweet.* It's supposed to be a really sweet film. I'm not sure I'm talking about the right movie. But what the hell—I'll go with it."

• *Hoffa*: The second of the three biographies. "Danny DeVito almost killed himself to get this made, so you know there's a lot of passion going in." "A David Mamet script and an Oscar-caliber performance by Jack Nicholson. Plus, I loved the trailer, so I have no doubt about its quality."

• *Home Alone 2*: "Goldman, are you seriously asking me to discuss the *quality* of this one? The first one was one of the greatest crowd pleasers ever; it does not go by any known rules. The truth? I hear this is better." "I'm guessing that every joke that worked the first time, you'll see it twice here. Everything he hit them with the first time, he'll clobber them with twice as hard here." Finally, a bit of wisdom I hadn't heard before: "Sequels have changed. You used to know, rule of thumb, that the second one would do a third less. But now—look at the *Die Hards* and the *Lethal Weapons*—sequels can do more. But they've got to be exactly like the original. When they go to a sequel, *people want comfort.*"

• *Lorenzo's Oil*: "It's about a couple with a sick kid, so it's going to have to get past the notion that it's a TV disease-of-the-week flick. But George Miller—the doctor, right?—hasn't made a clinker yet." (Aside: There are two Australian film directors named George Miller. One—the other one—had as his biggest hit *The Man From Snowy River*. This one—the medical man—has been quiet since *The Witches of Eastwick*. I actually know a producer who was deep in negotiations with one of them when he realized he was about to sign the wrong one. Don't ask me which—he's not sure. End of aside.) This movie stars Nick Nolte and Susan Sarandon, and I will make a based-on-nothing prediction: It's Sarandon's year to win the Oscar, and she will for *Lorenzo's Oil*.

• *Malcolm X*: "The controversial flick of the decade" is the feeling Out There. None of my sources had seen it, and interestingly enough, they ended up talking about its commercial chances more than its artistic merits. "I think its length will hurt it." "I think blacks will go—some of them many times—but I wonder about its crossover business." They all agreed that this, the third of the season's biographies, would be one where quality could be taken for granted. Personal note: I have seen it, and yes, it is more than three hours. Only it doesn't feel like it. I thought *Do the Right Thing* was a major film, but this leaves behind everything else Spike Lee has done. And if Denzel Washington doesn't get a Best Actor nomination, it will be the biggest heist since Landslide Lyndon Johnson's people fiddled with the ballot boxes decades ago in Texas.

• *The Muppet Christmas Carol*: Not many commented. "The Muppets haven't been expanding their audience base lately—if you liked the others, you'll like this."

• *Scent of a Woman*: "Marty Brest doesn't direct many movies—I think, his last two were *Beverly Hills Cop* and *Midnight Run*—and there's a strong feeling here we're talking about an excellent film." "I've seen it, and it's Al Pacino's best performance."

• *Toys*: "There is no way this can be a clinker. You've got Barry Levinson directing a script by Barry Levinson, in a comedy starring Robin Williams." "I love the trailer, and I've read it—this is not a piece of block-comedy material like *Good Morning, Vietnam*. Is that right? Did I use 'block comedy' correctly? Anyway, it's got a lot of different elements, and those are hard—there's always the danger of falling between stools. But everyone I know wants to see it."

• *Trespass*: "Walter Hill directing Ice T. That's all I know." That's all anybody knew. The secret film of the season. No one would even hazard a guess.

• *Used People*: "How can you beat that cast? Kathy Bates, Marcello Mastroianni, Shirley MacLaine? "I know it's going to be good. What I don't know is, is it going to be this year's *Fried Green Tomatoes*?"

So there we are. I've never felt like a shill for the industry before. I'm just hoping they're right. Of course, so are they. But this time, they feel confident. Hard as I tried, I couldn't get a snarl from anybody. One studio head summed it up: "Wonderful movies. Just wonderful movies." Then he paused: "God, I haven't been able to say that in years."

—NOVEMBER 16, 1992

REQUIEM FOR A HEAVYWEIGHT

Paris, Jan. 30 (AP)—The professional wrestler Andre Rene Roussimoff, a native of France who was known to fans as Andre the Giant, died this week, apparently of a heart attack. He was 46.

He was handsome once. I remember a photo he showed me, taken at a beach with some friends. Dark, good-looking kid, maybe 17. Big, sure—he said he was around six foot eight then and weighed 275—but that was before the disorder really kicked in. Acromegaly. Something goes haywire with the growth hormones. He was working as a furniture mover during the day, taking wrestling lessons at night, sleeping when he could.

At 25, he topped out, but I don't think he ever actually knew his size. I met him in England when he was playing the rhyme-loving Fezzik in *The Princess Bride*. I had written the novel and now the screenplay. This was in the summer of '86, and Andre's publicity listed him at seven foot five, 550 pounds. Close enough. All he was sure of was that he'd had pneumonia a little while earlier and had lost 100 pounds in three weeks in the hospital.

Gone now at 46, he was the most popular figure on any

movie set I've ever been on.

He was *very* strong. I was talking to an actor who was shooting a movie in Mexico. What you had to know about Andre was that if he asked you to dinner, he paid, but when you asked him, he also paid. This actor, after several free meals, invited Andre to dinner and, late in the meal, snuck into the kitchen to give his credit card to the maitre d'. As he was about to do this, he felt himself being lifted up in the air. The actor, it so happens, was Arnold Schwarzenegger, who remembers, "When he had me up in the air, he turned me so I was facing him, and he said, 'I pay.' Then he carried me back to the table, where he set me down in my chair like a little boy. Oh, yes, Andre was *very* strong."

When Arnold Schwarzenegger tells me someone is *very* strong, I'll go along with it.

Andre once invited Schwarzenegger to a wrestling arena in Mexico where he was performing in front of 25,000 screaming fans, and after he'd pinned his opponent, he gestured for Schwarzenegger to come into the ring.

So through the noise, Schwarzenegger climbs up. Andre says, "Take off your shirt; they are all crazy for you to take off your shirt. I speak Spanish." So Schwarzenegger, embarrassed, does what Andre tells him. Off comes his jacket, his shirt, his undershirt, and he begins striking poses. And then Andre goes to the locker room while Schwarzenegger goes back to his friends.

And it had all been a practical joke. God knows what the crowd was screaming, but it wasn't for Schwarzenegger to semi-strip and pose: "Nobody gave a s— if I took my shirt off or not, but I fell for it. Andre could do that to you."

Andre never knew what reaction he might cause in people. Sometimes children and grown-ups would see him and be terrified. Sometimes children would see him, shriek with glee, and begin clambering all over him as if the greatest toy imaginable had just been given them. And he would sit, immobile, as they roamed around him. Sometimes he'd put a hand out, palm up, and they'd sit there, for what they hoped would be forever.

Andre would never come out and say that wrestling might not be legit. He fought 300-plus times a year for about twenty years, and all he ever admitted was that he didn't like being in the ring with someone he thought might be on drugs. When he was in his prime, men who weighed 250 to 300 pounds would hurl themselves on him from the top of the ring, and he would catch them and not budge.

But even seven years ago, his body was betraying him. There is a scene at the end of *The Princess Bride* where Robin Wright—and yes, she is that beautiful—jumped out of the castle window, and Andre was to catch her at the bottom.

The shot was set up for Robin to be lifted just above camera range and then dropped into Andre's arms. Maybe a foot. Maybe two. But not much, and Robin was never heavy.

The first take, she was dropped and he caught her—and gasped, suddenly white like paper, and almost fell to his knees. His back was bad. And getting worse, and soon there would be surgery.

Andre once said to Billy Crystal, "We do not live long, the big and the small."

Alas.

—FEBRUARY 15, 1993

YEAR OF THE DOG

SCOPING THE OSCARS

Understand this about the Oscar nominees: They're *all* quality work. You may feel your favorites have been shafted, but the Academy members are not airheads. *How to Stuff a Wild Bikini* was not nominated back in '65, and no matter how much movies have slipped since then—and they're closing in on horrendous—it would not have snuck in this year either.

Still, there is some work that is so remarkable that no matter what the year, you can't do much besides stand in silence and give thanks that God, in Her wisdom, invented Talent. Following is a list of my personal favorites. (Billing alphabetical.)

1. Marlon Brando, *A Streetcar Named Desire*. The one that changed everything. Certainly the most important performance of the postwar era.

2. James Cagney, *White Heat*. One of our greatest actors in his greatest performance in the greatest gangster film ever made.

3. Bette Davis, *All About Eve*. "Fasten your seat belts;

it's going to be a bumpy night." Magical.

4. Robert De Niro, *Taxi Driver*. I don't think he's ever been better, which is saying a lot more than a little.

5. Katharine Hepburn, *The Philadelphia Story*. An amazing piece of work—even more amazing when you consider the quality of the rest of the cast: James Stewart won an Oscar for giving the *third* finest performance in the film.

6. Jack Nicholson, *Chinatown*. See it again; he's even better the fifth time.

7. Peter O'Toole, *Lawrence of Arabia*. The greatest epic—but it wouldn't have been without his acting as the rock-like core.

8. Michelle Pfeiffer, *The Fabulous Baker Boys*. She is the most brilliant young character actress we have; you cannot blame her for her genes. And she must never come down from that piano.

9. James Stewart, *It's a Wonderful Life*. Pick your own adjective and square it. He was still better.

10. Meryl Streep, *Silkwood*. Her most emotional, most moving work.

None of these performances won the Oscar. Cagney didn't even get nominated.

If I begin with a trick like that, there's a reason: These are the trickiest Oscars to predict within memory. Months ago, the wisdom was that there were three leaders: *A Few Good Men*, *Malcolm X*, and *Unforgiven*. *Malcolm* was the first to fall from favor, being replaced by *Howards End*. Then *A Few Good Men* began to lose a step. Then, oh then, came *The Crying Game*.

One of my informants complained, "No one's ever heard of so many of these people, I hope they give scorecards.

I can't remember when this has happened before, but the Academy is not made up of outsiders. This year, the mainstream turned against the mainstream."

Despite the overwhelming insecurity, my Wizards Out There were willing to guess. What follows is their (nervous) profundity.

BEST ACTOR

• Robert Downey Jr., *Chaplin*. "The nomination is his award."

• Clint Eastwood, *Unforgiven*. "The Academy has other ways to honor him—director, picture. They'll skip past him on this one."

• Al Pacino, *Scent of a Woman*. "An absolute lock to win."

• Stephen Rea, *The Crying Game*. "There's a craziness this year, and *The Crying Game* is the center of the storm."

• Denzel Washington, *Malcolm X*. "A while back, I thought he was unstoppable. Now he's practically out of it; I don't know why." "I know why he won't win: The movie stopped being *chic*."

Personal: Pacino, for two reasons. (1) He's been hosed more than anybody. (2) Pacino plays a blind man. The Academy loves that kind of thing—they think it's hard to play drunks or autistics. But it's the easiest thing in the world for a skilled actor. What's hard is being still. What's really hard is being still and being interesting at the same time. Hoffman was fine in *Rain Man*, but for me, *the* performance in that baby was given by Tom Cruise. He was the rock. Kevin Costner will never win a Best Actor award—until he plays an amputee.

BEST ACTRESS

• Catherine Deneuve, *Indochine*. "She was terrific, but if she wins, next they'll want the Louisiana Purchase back."

• Mary McDonnell, *Passion Fish*. "Lovely work." "Who saw the picture?"

• Michelle Pfeiffer, *Love Field*. "I didn't see it. Which is why she won't win." "Once again—who saw the picture?"

• Susan Sarandon, *Lorenzo's Oil*. "This was a top-notch movie, and her work was so quietly moving." "A solid second; that's not so terrible. If the picture had been a hit, she'd have taken it all."

• Emma Thompson, *Howards End*. "She's won every award so far; she'll win this too." "A lock—with an asterisk. The last three years, Brits have won Best Actor. If the Academy decides enough is enough, Sarandon could slip in."

Personal: Thompson is probably as much of a favorite as Pacino. But what's interesting this year is that none of the performances were in movies with wide audience appeal, usually a big plus for the Academy. *Howards End*, the most successful of the five, has been out a year, and it's taken in less in all that time than *The Bodyguard* did its first weekend.

Another clue that this is an unusual year is that the single most commercially valuable performance wasn't recognized: Sharon Stone in *Basic Instinct*. My feeling is, the movie wouldn't work with anyone else in the role. Granted, this is not the kind of movie the Academy tends to honor, but Julia Roberts was nominated for *Pretty Woman*, which is also not the kind of movie that the Academy tends to honor.

Strange things, indeed, are happening Out There.

Which brings me to *The Crying Game*. There has been a lot of coyness when people discuss this flick. "Skip the next paragraph if you don't want to know the secret." That kind of thing.

To which I say, horsepucky.

Penis, penis, penis, penis, penis. Jaye Davidson, who is rightfully up for Best Supporting Actor, has a penis. So does half of the rest of the world. The difference here is that he plays what you think is a woman until 69 minutes into the movie.

There. Secret out.

Now, why was I such a crummy spoilsport? (1) By the time you read this, the movie will have been playing in town well into its sixteenth week. If you haven't seen it by now, then you're not a movie fan, and you wouldn't have gone anyway. When does the statute of limitations on surprises run out? I say at sixteen weeks.

(2) I've seen the movie twice, once not knowing, and it's a far *better* movie if you know. Because *The Crying Game* has more script falseness than any quality movie I can think of. But once the secret is out, the heart of the flick is allowed to be seen—what the hell is love nowadays, anyway?—and the relationship after the penis shot is beautifully handled by writer-director Neil Jordan.

The movie was a commercial disaster in Britain; it was the sixty-seventh most popular movie of the year there. I spoke with two London film critics about it. The first said, "It got mixed reviews here. I went easy on it. I like Neil, and I didn't want to harm his slightly lame creation. I hated it when Stephen Rea, the IRA terrorist, got to London. I almost subtitled it 'A Pussycat Comes to Town.' "

The other critic was harsher: "The whole first third is

crap—an IRA terrorist out of Walt Disney. Let me change it slightly. Let's say a bunch of Ku Klux Klan members kidnap a black in Alabama. And before too many hours go by, the Klansman is so won over by the black, he turns to jelly. Would your audiences believe that? I don't think so. We know what terrorists do: They kill people. The IRA are terrorists. I wonder if you people would have thought so highly of the film if it had opened *after* the terrorist killed those people at the World Trade Center. Terrorists are not sweet, they are swine, and any attempt to say they're not is meretricious."

(3) The crucial reason for the movie's success is the shot of the penis. The camera pans down Davidson's body as he and Rea are about to make love; and there it is—gasp—a male member. Rea gets physically ill. If the shot had stopped at Davidson's navel, then cut to Rea gasping, "My God, you're a man," no one would have stood in line to see the movie.

I hope I'm *adding* to the commerciality of the movie. Miramax is a sensational company. And now that you know what is up there onscreen, I doubt that anything will keep you away.

BEST DIRECTOR

• Robert Altman, *The Player*. "Not much of a chance—he did good work, but it was a critics' picture."

• Martin Brest, *Scent of a Woman*. "I wish he worked more; when he does, it's good stuff. But I rate him third here."

• Clint Eastwood, *Unforgiven*. "I rated him even with Neil Jordan before he won the Directors Guild Award. Now I don't think anything can stop him." "Finally, they're honoring a great career."

• James Ivory, *Howards End*. "*The Crying Game* stole his spot."

• Neil Jordan, *The Crying Game*. "He could sneak in—it's not a Hollywood film, and this year it's obvious the Academy isn't very high on Hollywood films."

Personal: Eastwood. People connect him so strongly with just being an action star, they forget he's directed sixteen films, many of them wonderful: *Play Misty for Me, Bronco Billy,* and *Bird*, to select three favorites. I don't think of this as a career award. I think it's a case of, well, about time.

BEST PICTURE

• *The Crying Game*. "Logically, it should be *Unforgiven*. But I think the Academy genuinely wants to honor this film, and I think they will here." "Eastwood's too strong, but I would not keel over if this took it."

• *A Few Good Men*. "I feel it's just gone away in the minds of the voters."

• *Howards End*. "Tasteful, well done—but *The Crying Game* kills it." "This is not a strong year, so again, I would not keel over if this took it either."

• *Scent of a Woman*. "I just don't see it winning against this opposition." "Pacino would have to pull it across the line."

• *Unforgiven*. "Should." "A lock . . . no . . . half a lock—Goldman, use this: Half a lock is better than none."

Personal: Again, weak year, terrible year. *Unforgiven* was the leader, the only one people had genuine feeling for. One executive predicted, "This is going to be the lowest-rated Oscar show in memory."

But since it's unconstitutional to end a Hollywood piece on a downbeat, I'd like to wind this up by talking about a category I haven't before: Best Supporting Actor. (In the other support category, Judy Davis is the favorite for her work in *Husbands and Wives*.) What is unusual about the supporting-male category is that I can think of five actors who could have *won* . . . and they didn't even get nominated: Alec Baldwin, Al Freeman Jr., Tommy Lee Jones, Jack Lemmon, and Sydney Pollack.

The five who did, deservedly, get nominated—Jaye Davidson, Gene Hackman, Jack Nicholson, Al Pacino, and David Paymer—did some wonderful work.

And the winner is?

Let me quote one of my wise men: "If you want to bet, Hackman. But remember two things. First of all, the Academy *does* want to honor *The Crying Game*. But more important, we're in the *entertainment* business. So I say Davidson wins, and here's why: Half the town is dying to know what in hell he'll wear."

—MARCH 22, 1993

THE FOLLOWING WERE ACADEMY AWARD WINNERS FOR 1992:

Best Actor	*Al Pacino, Scent of a Woman*
Best Actress	*Emma Thompson, Howard's End*
Best Director	*Clint Eastwood, Unforgiven*
Best Picture	*Unforgiven*

CINEMA 66

≥

SCOPING THE CELLULOID OF SUMMER

No more shopping days till Christmas.

Readers of these occasional forays may remember that the holiday season is when the movie business goes nuts, cramming far too many flicks into those two weeks at the end of the year. Well, this summer they've gone mad, too. As I write this, there is no consensus on how many films will open, but the highest guess I've heard is—holding your breath?—*66*. Clearly, there is going to be a lot of falling by the wayside.

I have talked to the Masters, and all agree on one point: This, the summer of '93, is going to be, by very far, the highest-grossing in history.

But will it also be the most profitable? "These days, the key word is *profitability*," one of my informants opined. (I am closing in on the end of my fourth decade as a professional writer, and I've never used *opined* before. See? Happiness is just around the corner for us all, if we wait.) Opining further: "A lot of studios could gross a lot of money and still take some severe body hits. If *Jurassic Park* and *Last Action Hero* aren't enormous, the whole business will be damaged."

One of the clever things they've managed to do Out There to accommodate the coming flood is to alter the season. Summer used to be from Memorial Day to Labor Day. This year, it will have begun before you read this, with the opening, on May 7, of *Dave*—the only summer picture I've seen, and if you don't like it, you're wrong.

The following treatise does not deal with every one of the 66. I thought it might be interesting to catch the current wisdom on what the ten biggest pictures of the summer will be. Remember that for the most part, we are dealing in scuttlebutt. My experts have seen next to none of the crop. Alphabetically, then:

• *Cliffhanger*. "Great trailer, first action picture of the summer. Yes, I know it's Stallone, but if Eastwood can come back and Redford can come back, where is it written Sly can't?" "No, I'm not crazy, and I know that *Oscar* and *Stop! Or My Mom Will Shoot* won't have sequels. But the reason this will be big is simply amazing: I hear it's not that bad."

• *Dennis the Menace* (Mason Gamble, Walter Matthau, Christopher Lloyd). "It's John Hughes and Dennis the Menace. That's the whole thing. You don't even have to see the movie. You know everything about it just from that."

• *The Firm*. "It's going to explode. How can it not? Tom Cruise and the first John Grisham novel to hit the screen." "This is going to be gigantic, but there's an 'if.' It will be gigantic *if it's not too good*. Remember, this is summer; it's brainless time. If they haven't tried to make more of it than it is—just a potboiler—through the roof. If they tried to make it—spare me—*about* something, could be trouble."

• *The Fugitive*. "People seem to like these old TV series as movies. I think they'll like this." "It's Harrison Ford. Put him in *The Mosquito Coast*—a serious flick in which he was as good as he's ever been—no interest. But in an adventure film, he doesn't miss."

• *Hot Shots! Part Deux* (Charlie Sheen, Lloyd Bridges, Valeria Golino). "It's a sequel; people liked the first one; it's opening early." "It's that brainless thing that blooms in the summer. It will definitely be in the top ten and will get even fewer votes than *Dennis the Menace* come next Oscars."

• *In the Line of Fire* (Clint Eastwood, John Malkovich). "A perfect role for Clint. Plus, it may be the best movie of the summer. There are three with fantastic 'word,' and this is going to be the biggest." "It's an example of everything being right: the right kind of movie at the right time with the right talent. Unstoppable."

• *Jurassic Park* (Sam Neill, Laura Dern, Jeff Goldblum). "The second-biggest movie in history on a worldwide basis." "It could be a gigantic flop and still make the top ten. Top two." "One caveat. These last months of postproduction are essential, and Spielberg's a master at it. But he's been out of the country shooting *Schindler's List*. So George Lucas is helping. Fabulous talent no question, but his two best movies—*American Graffiti* and *Star Wars*—were edited by his ex-wife, Marcia Lucas. If I'm Universal, I've got to be wishing Steven was closer to home. Still, it probably won't matter—gotta see those dinos."

• *Last Action Hero* (Arnold Schwarzenegger, Austin O'Brien, Art Carney). I worked on this, so don't trust what follows. All I will say is that if it doesn't make this list come fall, Sony will hire the Japanese army to attack Southern California.

• *Made in America* (Whoopi Goldberg, Ted Danson). "The second with fantastic word." "All I know is this: The studio is so confident about what they've got, they're already signing up everyone for a sequel. I don't remember that happening before."

• *Super Mario Bros.* (Bob Hoskins, John Leguizamo, Dennis Hopper). "I don't know what it is, but my kid won't stop bugging me about it." "I don't know anything about it, but my kids do. And I wish they'd shut up about it." "It opens the same day as *Cliffhanger* and *Made in America*. And we're all going to be smiling. . . ."

The only three to make every list were *Jurassic Park*, *Last Action Hero*, and *Made in America*. The biggest four were predicted to be *The Firm, In the Line of Fire, Jurassic Park*, and *Last Action Hero*. Try and figure how that works when you're standing on line. I gave up on it yesterday.

The Masters were also wondering what was going to be this summer's surprise hit, like *Sister Act*. They should have asked me. It's going to be *Sleepless in Seattle* (Tom Hanks, Meg Ryan), directed by Nora Ephron—the third where word of mouth won't stop building. And that's, finally, why we go to a movie: Someone says, "Hey, it's good."

—MAY 17, 1993

CITY OF ANGLES

Yes, it was a wonderful summer for movies, but this year, movies were only the second-best product Hollywood gave us, the clear winner being . . . gossip. A legendary time. Like '61 Bordeaux, if you're into wine. Those of us who purchase *The New York Review of Books* not to read, but to conceal the tabloids, must light candles for the toilers at the *Star* and the *Enquirer*, praying they don't perish from overwork.

As a serious contemporary artist, I have spent these fortnights trying to find a vehicle that would best display the talents of Michael and Burt and Loni and Lady Fleiss. Chekhov seemed a good idea, what with the multitude of splendid roles, and Loni would definitely score in *The Cherry Orchard*, but I don't know about the rest. Probably I should let Mary Ann Madden run a casting contest and give a prize. In a few months, our lives will again be humdrum, overladen with Elvis sightings and Oprah weigh-ins, but for the moment . . . bliss.

They're pretty blissful Out There, too. In the May 17 issue of these pages, the experts predicted happiness—the biggest summer in history, they said, and right they were. But they were wrong more often than not as to which movies would break out.

Perhaps the most important date of the summer was August 6—well after the summertime madness. That was when *The Fugitive* opened, and it will likely total $200 million at the box-office before Ford stops running.

This seems to fly in the face of the studios' obsession to rush their product to the marketplace not when it's ready but when a holiday looms. One studio head, who was worried, said this: "There has always been a battle between the production end of the company and distribution. But now, more than ever, distribution is winning." And with a certain logic: If you have *Jurassic Park* or *Lethal Weapon 3*, you're pretty sure audiences are waiting for you.

Except the picture business is such an inexplicable quagmire; neither rules nor logic apply. Another executive said this: "Paramount rushed two movies this summer: *Sliver*, a disappointment, and *The Firm*, no comment necessary. Pictures come out and they do what they do, and that's that. You only have the one shot. You hope it's your best, but this is not an exact science."

But that doesn't stop them from trying to make scientific judgments, to learn from mistakes or, in the case of this summer, successes. These are the five Giant Apes of the past season. What do you think they think they have in common? Take your time.

The Firm. The Fugitive. In the Line of Fire. Jurassic Park. Sleepless in Seattle.

Got your answer? (Remember, no one is right, no one is wrong.) Okay. Enough. Here's the wisdom Out There. They all contain the following: STARS AS YOU WANT TO SEE THEM. Cruise and Ford and Eastwood and Spielberg and Hanks and Ryan. We want Tom Cruise when he makes us comfortable: playing a contemporary kid in a pickle. Not an Irish immigrant. Hanks when he's funny and sensitive, not as some Wall Street stud. Spielberg when he's scaring us, and on and on.

Before I give my guess as to what this means, add these facts to the equation: Foreign box-office now is often more than U.S. box-office. And overseas, they're much more star-happy than we are. Stars die a decade later over there.

I think salaries for the top stars have got to go up. I've been in the business long enough to remember being staggered when Burton and Taylor each got a million back in the late sixties. So what happens now that Tom Cruise already is reputed to get $12.5 million per film?

Does he get twenty next time at bat? Judging from the success of *A Few Good Men* and *The Firm*, $20 million would have been a steal. Pray tell me then, what does Kevin Costner's agent want after next year's *Wyatt Earp* goes through the roof?

Twenty-five million?

Thirty-five million?

I don't blame the stars for asking so much. All the studios have to do is say no. I'm real glad I don't have to pay them, but if I were a studio head, would I?

I wouldn't let them out of the room. No one has talked about this yet, so put it down as mad conjecture on my part. But who else but me and Suzy even begins to tell you these things?

Since I am into predicting, I am, with permission, going to blow a source's cover, because in the May 17 issue, Martin Shafer of Castle Rock made the most remarkable prediction I've ever heard: that *Jurassic Park* would be the *second*-largest grosser of all time. Attention must be paid. Even more amazing, Shafer's been saying that ever since Spielberg agreed to direct.

Not to be outdone, a few of my own: (1) Fall will be okay, not great. (2) Christmas will be good, not great. (3) Next summer will be—yawn—the biggest in history: No fewer than seven films are already being trumpeted as blockbusters. (4) When *A Perfect World* opens this November, Clint Eastwood will become, at the age of 63, the first star in history to head-line three consecutive $100 million grossers, according to my calculations.

(5) And in a paragraph all its own: Tom Hanks wins the Oscar next year for *Philadelphia*. A performance for the ages.

—SEPTEMBER 20, 1993

"STELLA!"

"Definitely the best movie year of the decade," one of my wizards was saying, which might have been a little like arguing that the Menendez kids were definitely more respectful than Lizzie Borden. "I'll bet if you ask around, you'll find a lot of agreement in town. It's a year we can be proud of."

I asked around and, yes, a surprising amount of agreement. Three examples. Writer of the year: "Zaillian. Terrific double." (*Searching for Bobby Fischer* and *Schindler's List.*) Director of the year: "Spielberg, obviously." (*Schindler* and *Jurassic.*) Performer of the year: "Tom Hanks." (*Sleepless* and *Philadelphia.*) "When has anyone done better? Ever."

And the biggest star?

Hmmmm.

Lest this seem a frivolous question (and it is), know that Out There, it is taken verrry seriously. "Of *course* I think about it a lot," said one studio exec. "I guess wrong, I can lose my job. There are genuine financial considerations too. Put this in caps, Bill: THESE PEOPLE GET PAID MORE FOR ONE PICTURE THAN CLARK GABLE EARNED IN HIS ENTIRE CAREER."

Last December, the common wisdom was this: Arnold

on top. Half a step behind, Costner. With these three dead-heating next in line: Cruise, Gibson, and Roberts. How have they fared?

Schwarzenegger was the most bulletproof performer in memory. Not hype, that. His prior four films had taken in *way* over a billion dollars at box-offices around the world. And for your viewing pleasure in 1993: *Last Action Hero*.

As one who toiled on that baby, two things: It's a lot better than you may have been led to believe, and it isn't remotely the stiff it has been touted to be. We are not smelling *Ishtar* here: *Hero* will take in more than $125 million worldwide. But it was wildly hyped and wildly rushed, and was easily the loudest disappointment of the year.

And the quietest disappointment of the year? Shhhh. It just opened, and no one's talking about it here yet. But they sure are Out There, and they have no answers as to why *A Perfect World* is the stunning commercial failure that it is. Good reviews, a good picture, Eastwood directing and co-starring, and Costner giving the performance of his career.

So are the golden duo a bit tarnished? "Silly to deny it," a top agent said. Are their careers irreparably damaged? "Not remotely . . . assuming their next movies do well. Try and remember two things: Fans are always in flux, and John Travolta." (Explanation: Travolta, after *Saturday Night Fever* and *Grease*, was as hot as anybody.)

Quickly now, the trailing three. Gibson made one movie this year, *Man Without a Face*, and it did only okay. "Wrong. It doesn't count," explained another agent (not Gibson's). "It was almost an art film. Like *Hamlet*, how it did at the box-office had no effect on his commercial appeal, which is enormous. I think he's the biggest star."

"Roberts is No. 1 in my book," says a different agent.

"Young, the only woman, mysterious, we care about her. And Pelican Brief is going to be enormous." (It took in more than $16 million in its first weekend, proving that her absence from films has only made her bigger.)

Cruise was anything but absent. He had two films, both giant successes—*A Few Good Men* and *The Firm*. "T.C. is *the* star now," says yet another agent. "Not even open to argument."

So which of the five is the biggest? The answer is . . . .

Hmmmm . . . .

The answer is *Harrison Ford*. Said another wise man: "He has been in more big hits than anyone, and I would rather have him than anyone."

The picture should be coming clear: There is a certain disagreement among the powerful people Out There. And is anything unusual about this? Actually, yes. Because more or less traditionally in the history of sound, there has been *a* biggest star. Sixty years ago, it was Will Rogers. He stayed on top one year. Two stars have held off the enemy for five consecutive years: Bing Crosby in the forties, and in the eighties, Burt Reynolds. Redford was a triple defender in the seventies. Doris Day the decade prior. Shirley Temple ruled the thirties, four years in a row. What's informative about these folks is what they say about what *we* wanted to see then.

And what do we want to see now? Nobody knows—our interests clearly are spread. We have six stars lunging for the finish line in a race that's too close to call. This year or next, one will win.

Eventually, of course, all will lose. We will grow bored, turn our backs, find new loves. But this is holiday time, so to each of the six, let us pledge not just love but love undying. I will if you will.

—JANUARY 3, 1994

OSCARS WILD

Will the Academy Take Steven Spielberg Seriously This Year?

Just as Santa had his fifteen minutes of fame in December, we are now awaiting Oscar's time. In two days, the nominations will be there for all of us to see and denounce. So let's take a breath while we can, and answer a few questions about Ye Grande Event in general and, more particularly, what the nominations can tell us about the eventual winners.

• Do the Oscars really, really, truly matter?

"More than you know . . . , " as the song says. And they matter in three very different ways. Fans get a chance to be critics and act superior and, more important, have something to talk about to forget it's February. The Oscars matter to the studios for the proper reason: money. If a movie is fairly new, such as *In the Name of the Father* or *Philadelphia* or *The Piano* or *Schindler's List*, millions of additional dollars will accrue as the film unspools across the country and the world.

But you have to understand something about those in the pit—well, at least many of them; well, at least, me—we are dogged by the fact that what we do for a living isn't a very grown-up way to spend our days.   We role-play, put on makeup, tell stories, all to try to please you sitting out there in the dark—*but it's not real work*.   A research scientist doesn't feel what we do.   Bankers and dentists would surely find such sentiments bizarre.   My God, funeral-parlor directors know their jobs can be crucial, while those of us in show biz know that we are toys to be picked up and admired for a while and disposed of as childhood recedes.

For us, then, the Oscars are not about finance or frivolity—in the end they are only about one thing: validation.

• Is the voting honest, and is it serious?

Yes and yes.   In the old days of true studio power, you voted for whom you were told, or the studio picked up your ballot and marked it for you.   No longer.   Most of the people I know vote their conscience, always with the caveat that if a friend or, more usually, an enemy is there, *get him*.   But most of us ponder and argue and shift and eventually make our decisions.

• Does the right movie or individual win?

Never or always, depending on whom you were rooting for.   This is the hardest point for most people to accept, but *we are not dealing with higher mathematics here*.   I think Graham Greene was the greatest novelist in English this century.   Never won the Nobel Prize.   Pearl Buck won the Nobel Prize.   Personally, I find that egregious and stupefying, but the Nobel committee found it swell, and it matters more.   There have been a lot of Oscar decisions I find dubious.   Doesn't make me wrong, doesn't make me right.   All the Oscars can tell us that has any meaning is this: *They reflect how the Academy voters felt that year*.

• Does it matter who the particular nominees are, in the sense of does one nominee affect the others' chances?

My particular feeling is that it matters more than anything. And to try to make sense of that, we are going to spend the rest of class discussing what is shaping up as the single most controversial category this year, that of Best Director.

There are two locks—*The Piano's* Jane Campion and Steven Spielberg, the man behind *Schindler's List*. They are special talents. They live in different worlds, geographically (she is from New Zealand and lives in Australia) and in every other way. And it would be a remarkable upset if neither of them won.

Campion is the most honored director this year, both at Cannes and in the majority of the year-end critics' polls. "Hers is the achievement," said a fellow director. "Spielberg started with a wonderful book on a unique piece of subject matter—it's really the only happy Holocaust story. But how you begin with nothing and end with *The Piano* just amazes me. I don't know how she did it, but she's going to be a major figure for years to come."

But everyone who has ever been nominated for an Oscar brings baggage along, and besides her talent, Campion brings some baggage that is very powerful indeed. I'm sure this will not shock either her or anyone who knows her well, but Campion is a woman. Her sex is her secret weapon.

Because Hollywood is *desperate* to honor a woman. (The recent embarrassing "Year of the Woman" hype is just an indication.) "I'll tell you what makes her particularly appealing." This from a *"Premiere* Magazine Power 100" type. "Penny Marshall and Barbra Streisand do outstanding work. But it's *standard*. I don't mean that as a knock—*Casablanca* is my favorite film, and *that's* standard directing, too. Campion isn't like anybody else. You get the feeling this is the start of a major career and you may as well honor it now. And remember, women *love* this movie. More even than men. And a lot of people want to have a woman win who is not just a woman but a woman with gifts that are different and, well, *female*. No man alive could have directed *The Piano*."

Steven Spielberg doesn't need an introduction, but let's give him one anyway. He has, with his double of *Jurassic Park* and *Schindler's List*, become the first directing star since Hitchcock. The only other director to achieve such prominence in the sound era was Cecil B. De Mille. But De Mille had a radio show; Hitch worked the tube. Spielberg has done it only with films.

And he is, I think, in the Hollywood sense, the most important director of the past quarter-century. This era began with *Jaws* in 1975, which initiated the time of The Blockbuster. No other figure has understood that strange form as well as he. Spielberg directed the two top-grossing films of all time, *E.T.* and *Jurassic Park*. Amazing. Even more amazing is this, as reported by a studio executive: "Take away *E.T.* and *Jurassic Park*, and he's *still* the most successful director of all time." And there is still more. No producer has ever been as successful. No studio head has ever been as successful. In the past 60 years, no *star* has ever been as successful. Spielberg is simply the most successful human being ever to set foot on a soundstage.

But he has never won the Oscar.

• Should he have won?

Absolutely. Any director who has given us *Jaws*, *Close Encounters of the Third Kind*, *Raiders of the Lost Ark*, and *E.T.* can hold his head very high.

• Is it jealousy that turns people away?

Personally, I think so. But a lot of people Out There don't see it that way. Said an Oscar-winning figure, "I think it's the same as Michael Crichton winning the Pulitzer Prize. Steven does what he does better than anybody. But why does

he deserve any serious attention? If the movies weren't so popular, no one would give them a second thought.   Chris
Columbus has just directed three of the most popular movies of
all time [*Home Alone, Home Alone 2, Mrs. Doubtfire*]. Do I have
to start hearing the same s— about him when *Home Alone 3*
goes through the roof?" Another correspondent weighed in
thusly: "Spielberg's becoming the Susan Lucci of Oscar nominations."

• Has this kind of thing ever happened before?

All the time.

The fact is, *many* of the greatest directors never won the
Best Director award. Example: Charlie Chaplin. Sure, a lot of
his work was before the Oscar era. But nothing wrong with
City Lights, Modern Times, The Great Dictator, Monsieur Verdoux,
or *Limelight*. (Chaplin never even got nominated for any of
them.) Example: Alfred Hitchcock. Example: Howard Hawks.
Example: Orson Welles. (If you want a contemporary, how
about Stanley Kubrick? He had *Dr. Strangelove, 2001*, and *A
Clockwork Orange* in a row, and came up empty.)

• Why do people feel Spielberg has been unjustly
treated?

It began with his not even getting a nomination for
Jaws. He got a nomination for his next film, *Close Encounters of
the Third Kind*, but lost to Woody Allen for *Annie Hall*. He got
a nomination for *Raiders of the Lost Ark*, but lost to Warren
Beatty for *Reds*.

Then, oh then, came *E.T.*

There was tremendous speculation that night as to
whether he would win or not. The enemy was *Gandhi*, directed
by Richard Attenborough. Attenborough won. For Spielberg's
enthusiasts, there was now blood on the moon.

My feeling is that there may well have been an over-looked director that night, but it sure wasn't Spielberg. For me, both *E.T.* and *Gandhi* were beautifully directed, and it comes down to which moved you more. But if ever two directors were comfortable, they had to have been Attenborough and Spielberg: They were working in areas of their greatest strength—the pitch was right down Broadway. Why? Because Attenborough was aflame with a twenty-year dream that landed right in the center of his liberal imagination, and Spielberg was dealing with childhood fantasy.

But there was another director nominated that night—Sydney Pollack. Who had done close to two decades of fine films. Who had never won. And who is wonderful with actors and can do action and can sure do drama—but who has no skill at comedy. And all he directed that year was *Tootsie*, now and forever one of the greatest comedies. I would argue then that if anybody should have been recognized for achievement in direction, Pollack had one hell of a case. He could have directed *Gandhi.* He could have directed *E.T.* But neither Attenborough nor Spielberg could have come close to *Tootsie*.

Did Pollack get screwed? Nope. He just lost to Attenborough.

Nutshelling it then, whether Spielberg wins this year or not is of little significance in either boosting his price or pasting him up there with the immortals. He has already done far more than enough to ensure a place in movie history, and history will take him up eventually and judge him in its very slow way. Hell, Orson Welles just might be considered the greatest director *ever*, and guess what—he never had a hit.

Arguably, the third-best-received movie was *The Age of Innocence*, directed by Martin Scorsese, and by adding his name to the two front-runners, we enter into complexity. He is pretty close to a lock, and the movie will surely win several acting nominations. Scorsese is famous for his work with actors.

And a lot more. There is no such thing as a "greatest living American director," but if a poll were taken today, Scorsese would probably win. And the baggage that he brings to the party is this: Like Spielberg, he has never won. His first great film was *Taxi Driver*. John Avildsen won that year for *Rocky*. Scorsese didn't get nominated. He did get nominated for *Raging Bull*, but lost to Robert Redford, who directed *Ordinary People*. Scorsese has been nominated twice more since, but no brass ring.

And whom does he affect in the voting?

Said one agent, "Obviously Spielberg, but I don't think it's a knife in the heart. This is not great Scorsese, it's just different Scorsese. And the movie is a financial flop. People don't know that because they don't want to hear it. More perfume has been tossed at this baby than any other, not counting *Schindler*. He hurts Spielberg, no question. And if it were just the three of them, and Campion won, it wouldn't be a surprise."

But, of course, it isn't just the three of them, and the fourth director who is favored to win a nomination is Jim Sheridan for *In the Name of the Father*. "He kills Campion. No. Nora Ephron, if she gets nominated for *Sleepless in Seattle*, *she* kills Campion. 'Two women,' enough voters would think. 'That's plenty already. Don't want to overdo this woman thing.' Sheridan, though, he definitely damages her, because the films are in one sense so similar—both low-budget, both foreign but English-speaking, both really art films. And voters can say, 'That's plenty already; don't want to overdo this art-film thing.' "

More quickly now, some other potential nominees. Robert Altman, who directed *Short Cuts*. His baggage is like Scorsese's—a critically acclaimed director who has never won. "I don't think he's going to get nominated. And if he is nominated, I guarantee you he isn't going to win. But at the same time, if he is nominated, sure, he hurts Spielberg."

Jonathan Demme: *Philadelphia*. "He really hurts Spielberg. Out Here, we think he's as good as anybody. Critics have loved him for years, and with *The Silence of the Lambs*, we like to think he is now one of us. The best thing for Steven here is that Demme just won for *Silence*. But Oliver Stone won twice, so it can happen and just might here—the picture is doing more business than anybody thought."

Andrew Davis for *The Fugitive*. This was probably more people's favorite movie than any other. (Davis fans such as myself were not surprised—*Under Siege*, starring Steven Seagal, was a wonderful flick, which is a little more difficult than directing a wonderful flick with Laurence Olivier.) "He doesn't affect either Campion or Spielberg—the nomination is his award. It certifies that he is on the top of the A list. Same thing, really, with Wolfgang Petersen for *In the Line of Fire*. Terrific commercial movies do not generally win awards."

James Ivory: *The Remains of the Day*. "There is always a Merchant/Ivory slot. A tasteful, well-crafted small film. Except this year, with Sheridan and Campion in the Merchant/Ivory slot, Merchant/Ivory may get shut out of the Merchant/Ivory slot. But this definitely hurts Campion."

When the nominations are announced, if Altman, Demme, and Scorsese are the other three, Spielberg is vulnerable. If the other three are Ephron, Ivory, and Sheridan, Campion is dead in the water. The fact of one nominee's affecting all the others is not just true here, it is true of every category, and it is true every year, and it can be interesting trying to mix and match and outguess the Academy.

You can usually come close to figuring winners from the nominees because everyone brings some baggage. It's never a case of someone's being "better," because "better" doesn't exist.

Two of my favorite actors, Paul Newman and Al Pacino, both deservedly won Best Actor awards. And I would argue that their work in *The Color of Money* and *Scent of a Woman* was their *worst* in nominated performances. (Think about it: *The Hustler* and *Cool Hand Luke* and *The Verdict* and *The Godfather, Part II* and *Serpico* and *Dog Day Afternoon*.) When they finally won, history was on their side. It is on Spielberg's now. Sex is all that can stop him.

He is the absolute overwhelming favorite. "I think the biggest we've had in maybe twenty years. Since Coppola with *Godfather*. Now, *that's* one you can't argue about—great, great directing." I agree. Fabulous. (For the young who are up past their bedtime, Coppola lost.)

—FEBRUARY 14, 1994

THE FOLLOWING WERE ACADEMY AWARD WINNERS FOR 1993:

Best Actor	*Tom Hanks, Philadelphia*
Best Actress	*Holly Hunter, The Piano*
Best Director	*Steven Spielberg, Schindler's List*
Best Picture	*Schindler's List*

THE OTHER ENVELOPES, PLEASE

THE TROUBLE WITH OSCAR NIGHT

The critics do not get it. Great television—and no, I have not been drinking—is, as we all know, rare. And I am not referring to Edward R. Murrow beginning the downslide of Joe McCarthy or Neil Armstrong goofing around on the moon. Those are choice moments, to be sure, but aberrations only. One cannot count on them.

But baby, you can always count on the Academy Awards, which is, along with the Miss America contest, the Everest of achievement in this country. (Yes, I have a bias. I once worked on one and judged the other and count both gigs among the giddy aesthetic experiences of my lifetime.)

My need to defend the Oscar show peaked when *USA Today* reported that Macaulay Culkin had backed out of giving the visual-effects award. (Elijah Wood and a dinosaur gave it.) Neither Mac nor his pop was treated with kindness. But why criticize them at all when they are merely part of the great tradition of the awards? Realize something: All the performers you see have multiple agents toiling on their behalf. As one of my correspondents explained, "Every presentation is a career move."

The year I helped write the show, I remember, the presenter of the screenwriting awards withdrew at the last minute. The producer had tried a fast patch job. I asked him if he'd had any luck. He began, pale and trembling, to imitate the star. (It was Yul Brynner.) "You want I geeve the *writing* awards? I am great star, and you offer me the fokking *writers*? You want me to geeve award, I geeve award. I geeve Best Peec-ture award. I geeve Best Actor. I am insulted. Gooood-bye." Eventually, Jack Lemmon did the job, and we were grateful. Lemmon, Walter Matthau, Charlton Heston, and a few others could always be counted on to come in and help.

When I was there, it was a television show about the movies done in a legitimate theater. You cannot conceive the potential for union trouble. It is an amazingly difficult show to pull off, but each year, somehow, it is done—and each year, the critics carp.

It is tacky, they say. It is tasteless. But it's the Oscar show; it's *supposed* to be tacky and tasteless. And mainly, the critics jump on the length. I dozed off, it was so slow, they say. They are only 180 degrees wrong. Now, there *is* a problem with the show—I never said it was perfect, just great—and here it is: *The trouble with the Oscar show is that it is too short.*

Think of the pleasures before us if they would forget about the money they get from commercials shown before midnight in the East and just let it roll. *No limitations on star speeches!* My God, give Richard Gere twenty minutes and maybe his thoughts *could* influence China. If Marlon Brando had known he could perorate like Caesar, he might have shown up in person to harangue us and not sent Sacheen Littlefeather. If Sally Field had been able to take her time, surely she would have segued into coloratura, such was her joy. Imagine yourself at 2:45 AM, desperate to stay awake because they haven't sung the fifth nominated song yet, much less gotten to Best Picture.

This year's edition was, as they all are, splendid. It had a dollop of bad taste, it had surprise, and, of course, the best medicinal movie won. The Academy has traditionally been a sucker for such stuff—medicinal movies are not so much movies that you like as movies that are supposed to make you feel better—and the recent honor roll is long. *Chariots of Fire, Out of Africa, Gandhi, The Last Emperor*—these are terrific pictures, understand. But, like Oskar Schindler, they are also extremely long on nobility.

The surprise of the night was Anna Paquin's winning Best Supporting Actress. The explanation might just be this: Out There, *The Age of Innocence* was not much beloved, so that damaged Winona Ryder. No one saw *Fearless*, so forget Rosie Perez. No one dared vote for Emma Thompson or Holly Hunter in this category, lest they win two and set a troubling precedent. I suspect the voters threw up their collective hands and said, "Oh, let someone else decide. I'm voting for the kid. She has no chance of winning." Strange forces shape our lives. My own awards, in no order whatsoever:

- BEST LINE READING: "I don't care." said by Tommy Lee Jones in *The Fugitive*, after Harrison Ford has informed him he is innocent of murdering his wife.

- BEST SCENE: When screenwriter Quentin Tarantino has Christopher Walken interrogate Dennis Hopper in *True Romance*.

- WORST SCENE: Schindler's farewell in *Schindler's List*. Amazing in a movie of this quality.

- BEST SEQUENCE: *A Perfect World*. The fifteen or so minutes toward the end when Kevin Costner is with the wonderful actress Mary Alice and her family.

- BEST EXAMPLE OF SHEER BLINDING STAR POWER: Tom

Cruise, at the climax of *The Firm*, somehow convincing the Mafia chieftains that what they really ought to be upset about is overbilling.

• SILLIEST SCENE: Sam Neill in the tree in Jurassic Park telling the kids that sure, it's okay to pet the dino. Never mind if the beast doesn't like it. What if it does like it and licks them gratefully? Its tongue alone could knock the tree down.

• BEST OSCAR CATEGORY EVER: Supporting Actor this year (Leonardo DiCaprio for *What's Eating Gilbert Grape?*, Ralph Fiennes for *Schindler's List*, Tommy Lee Jones for *The Fugitive*, John Malkovich for *In the Line of Fire*, Pete Postlethwaite for *In the Name of the Father*). All five would have won in ordinary vintages. (And please don't let anything bad ever happen to Leonardo DiCaprio.)

• BEST MOVIE FOR BUDDING SCREENWRITERS TO STUDY: *Free Willy* is absolutely ordinary until the kid looks toward the camera and says, "We gotta free Willy." After which, the movie is on rails. No other movie this year so clearly demonstrates the irresistible power of narrative.

• MOVIE REMEMBERED MOST AFFECTIONATELY TEN YEARS FROM NOW: *Groundhog Day*.

• BEST MOVIE: *What's Eating Gilbert Grape?* In a cakewalk.

Enough. There is a rumor that winter may be over. Go grab some sun while you can—the summer blockbusters are on the horizon. See you in the popcorn line.

—APRIL 4, 1994

YABBA-DABBA-DOO

THE CAN'T-MISS CELLULOID SUMMER

You *will* go to the movies this summer—something you seem to have forgotten how to do so far this year. On a happy July weekend, the top movies together can gross $120 million. One recent Friday to Sunday, the total was less than a third of that. Personally, I applaud your lapse. I cannot remember four months that were so dreary. Not only have American films been awful, they have been timid. If the Oscars were held today, nothing would win.

The theater exhibitors are in despair, too. Now, admittedly, that's their normal state, but usually it's because many of the imminent summer movies are obvious bombs simply waiting to be dropped. Summer 1994, however, will be the biggest in history. But *too many* successful films are about to be released, and the owners don't have enough theaters to show them in. Which, in turn, means that hits will get "dumped" (i.e., hurried off screens so the owners can honor previous commitments) as never before.

What follows is a list of movies that at least some of the Powers That Be feel have a shot at reaching $100 million in box-office gross. (Last summer, there were five: *Jurassic Park*,

The Fugitive, The Firm, Sleepless in Seattle, and *In the Line of Fire.*) To achieve that kind of popularity, a movie needs two things: appeal to a very broad audience and repeat business (people going back two and three times, as kids did to *Jurassic* and young women did to *Sleepless*). This year, there are—gasp—*fifteen* movies that hope to fill the bill. And what makes this summer freaky is that none of the fifteen feels like a *Heaven's Gate.* The conventional wisdom is that they will all do $50 million-plus.

Now this, of course, is madness. Studio executives need red ink (without failures they'd have no one to hate). But today, at least, *blissful* sums up their mood. Understand, of course, that everything that follows is hunch-playing. I simply asked studio executives, directors, and agents which movies might top the glorious $100-million benchmark. With few exceptions, these movies have not been seen by people outside the studios that are releasing them. And please remember that last year at this time, it was even money that *Last Action Hero* (which I worked on) would pummel *Jurassic.*

Who will soar this summer? Who will crash and burn? We'll all be smart come Labor Day. Here are the hopeful fifteen, in order of their scheduled openings (the names in parentheses are the most compelling reasons behind the hunches). Let's get started.

May 20: ***Maverick*** (Mel Gibson). "A lock 100 [million], Mel gets to be Mel." "Yes. Brilliantly positioned—first movie out of the chute, and the second weekend is Memorial Day." "Great concept—and it's not a Western. It's *Lethal* out West." I am involved with this effort, so I cannot comment on its quality. But I have seen it, and I promise that Jodie Foster does not destroy her career. Think Jean Arthur.

May 25: ***Beverly Hills Cop III*** (Eddie Murphy). In at least one way, the most interesting story of the summer. "Will breeze past 100. Eddie is back in the part that made him Eddie." But a majority strongly disagreed. "He was a phenomenon, no question. From *Saturday Night Live* to *48 Hrs.* Big hit. Then *Trading Places.* Not just a hit, but now he's a critics' darling. Then *Beverly Hills Cop.* Has anybody ever started faster? And what was he, 23? But that was ten years ago. This ain't the eighties anymore." "We know too much about him now. We know he's not the sweet, naive kid we wanted him to be. I think he is one of the two big summer stars whose careers have crested." (We'll come to the other one soon.)

May 27: **The Flintstones** (TV series). The most hotly disputed. "I don't know anything about it, but I don't have to know anything about it. It is a lock. Those old TV series have somehow become our mythology. People just love them. Could be awful, and it would do 100." "It will open huge, and it will die. That first weekend, half the assholes in America will be running around going, 'Yabba-dabba-doo.' But here's what everyone's forgotten: *The series was never that big.*" "Great concept—I'm not sure yet about the execution."

Personal aside: If last year's summer motto was STARS AS YOU WANT TO SEE THEM, this year it's CONCEPT AND EXECUTION. I hope that makes sense to you, because I didn't have the heart to ask what those words mean Out There this time around. For 50 years, I have been trying not to raise my hand as studio executives talked to me about the importance of a character's "arc." It sounds so obvious, I'm embarrassed to ask what they mean. Or maybe I'm terrified of finding out. Anyway, *execution, arc,* and *concept* are very much words of the moment.

June 3: **Renaissance Man** (Penny Marshall). Total ignorance of this one. Still, great expectations. "I think she might be the most commercial woman director ever." "I just get the feeling that Penny and Danny DeVito are going to be fun to be with."

June 10: *City Slickers II* (Billy Crystal) "Sequels are losing steam out here, but I hear it's testing sensationally." "For a sequel to work, it has to have something new, like Connery in the third *Indiana Jones*. This one doesn't have that. But I hear it's testing sensationally. I think everybody has heard it's testing sensationally."

June 17: *Wolf* (Jack Nicholson). One of the mysteries. "It was pulled from spring, Columbia said, because it was so terrific they wanted to play it in summer. May I tell you that no one above the age of 3 believes that? It was pulled because it wasn't ready. But it might be now." "I think Nicholson as a werewolf has great appeal." "I think Nicholson as a werewolf has zero appeal. I think Nicholson as *anything* has zero appeal—unless they want to see the film anyway. In which case he is gold."

June 17: *Getting Even With Dad* (Macaulay Culkin). The other falling star. "If this had come out after *Home Alone*, yes. Not now." "He's not a little kid anymore. No. Wrong. What am I saying? Of course he's still a little kid. He's just not the *same* little kid."

June 24: *Wyatt Earp* (Kevin Costner). "It could be *The Godfather* out West. It's the one I most want to see." "What is it, three hours long? And when did Larry Kasdan want to direct a commercial movie?"

June 24: *The Lion King* (Disney animation). King of the hill. "That's a stupid question: Is it going to do 100 million? There's only one subject for debate: Will it do *200* million?" "You know and I know this is a bullshit business. You pound your chest and wave your dick, but mostly you don't have the goods. They wouldn't be hyping it the way they're hyping it if they didn't have the goods." "The biggest star this summer is Disney animation. I don't think anything like that has happened."

June 29: *I Love Trouble* (Julia Roberts). "*Yes.* Heeeeere's Julia, all cheery and bright in a romantic comedy." "People keep expecting her to slip, but she doesn't—still, it would be nice if she got in a good picture every so often."

July 6: *Forrest Gump* (Tom Hanks). General feeling: This and *Wyatt Earp* could be the two highest-quality movies. "The sleeper of the summer." "Absolutely the sleeper of the summer." My favorite bit of reasoning: Tell me, pray, how a movie starring Tom Hanks, whose last three times out were *A League of Their Own*, *Sleepless in Seattle*, and *Philadelphia*—and directed by Robert Zemeckis, who ranks with Steven Spielberg and Ivan Reitman in terms of money—could possibly be a *sleeper*? One studio exec I asked said—curtly, I might add— "Goldman, you just don't understand anything about selling a picture." He's right.

(A word here about sleepers. Last year, *Sleepless in Seattle* came from nowhere to claim the championship. A producer on the Sony lot at the time said this: "They didn't have a sleeper—they just did a lot of work to make people *think* they did. The movie was testing in the mid-90s—even little boys liked it. They took advantage of the title to make the connection." Said a peer, "Nowadays, a sleeper is something the studios didn't think was any good, and to their dismay, it turns out it *is* good and they don't want anyone to bring expectations. But the truth is this: The day of the major studio sleeper is over." I absolutely agree. And this summer's major studio sleeper will be *Little Big League* (starring Timothy Busfield).

July 15: *True Lies* (Arnold). The last time Schwarzenegger and James Cameron worked together, they brought us *Terminator 2*. But a lot of doubt here. Not *if* it would do well, but *when*. It has been delayed once. The feeling was that it could be again. But no one wanted to open against it. "It had better do well—the budget could feed Central America."

July 22: **The Client** (John Grisham). "Yes, if it's great execution." "Julia barely made 100 with the last Grisham [*The Pelican Brief*]. I don't see it here."

July 29: **The Mask** (Jim Carrey). If you wonder how Hollywood keeps the Valium industry profitable, consider Jim Carrey. As the white guy on *In Living Color*, he was not widely known before *Ace Ventura*. Now a potential member of the elite. "This had a great trailer. Yes." "I *love* him. Of course, if this stiffs, I may not return his calls—a *joke*. I always return calls. Shit, Goldman, I even returned yours."

August 5: **Clear and Present Danger** (Harrison Ford). There is no true way of measuring star power. But this might come close. "It's a sequel to *Patriot Games*, which did over 80. But that came after *Regarding Henry*. This follows *The Fugitive*. If it breaks 100, credit that solely to Mr. Ford."

Perhaps more shocking than the movies listed are those that didn't make the cut, any of which could break through. Oliver Stone has a movie about violence (*Natural Born Killers*) and Rob Reiner has a comedy (*North*) and Andy Bergman has a comedy (*It Could Happen to You*). And John Hughes has a movie about a kid (*Baby's Day Out*), and there's also *Lassie* and *Black Beauty*, and Alec Baldwin is *The Shadow*, and *The Cowboy Way* might make it and *Angels in the Outfield* will make it, and there's *Blown Away*, and *Speed* is going to explode.

For Hollywood, summer has traditionally been in two parts: from Memorial Day through the Fourth of July, then the rest. And traditionally, the summer has been frontloaded. Get the monsters out early and let them run.

But this year, that's just not true. If you're Mr. Universal and you're selling *Flintstones*, well, it's not that difficult, in May, to round up 2,000 theaters, the number you need to open wide these lunatic days. But it's not at all easy to do it in July, if a lot of earlier summer hits are still playing.

And when a movie gets dumped while it still has appeal, you're talking $10 million—maybe $25 million—that isn't going to be earned. The battle for the theaters will become merciless. Lifelong friendships will end. Phone lines will steam. Might make a good movie—I like the concept. But I guess a lot depends on execution. (If you find an arc here, keep it to yourself.)

—MAY 23, 1994

LOOKING FOR NO. 1

Who's the biggest star in Hollywood? A clue: not Kevin Costner. Or Julia Roberts. And why does it matter?

This is the second report on *the* question that must be answered before America can take its rightful place as moral leader to the world: *Who is the biggest star in movies?* Although stars have always been essential to studios, it's probably safe to say that in the nineties, this is more true than ever.

1. Because costs will not stop rising.

2. Because expectations rise alongside.

3. By far the most important reason: *because there are so few of them*.

Why else do we know so much about Cindy and Linda and Claudia and Paulina and Kate? We didn't know that much about Cheryl, the first modern supermodel, and she was a lot more interesting. (More beautiful too. Still is.) But today, there is a gigantic media machine that has been erected solely to belch out star crap. Airtime and print columns need to be filled with *something*. And much as we may adore them, we can only digest so much about Sly or Mel or Harrison.

Before we get to the countdown, a couple of comments about '94: (1) In terms of the number of quality films, it has been the finest year in decades. (2) The latest fad. And no, it isn't science fiction or action-adventure. Give up? *Best-selling novels.* The phenomenal start for *Interview With the Vampire* ices it. Think of Grisham and Clancy and Crichton and now Rice. Grisham got paid $6 million for *A Time to Kill*, and you know what I think?

A steal.

Both Grisham and Crichton will have new novels finished in the next few months, and maybe one of them breaks the $10-million barrier. Sound crazy? If they had gotten $10 million for their last three, or Clancy had, the movies would still have made fortunes. These people are, right now, very big stars.

And please remember the definition of a star: someone who can *open* a picture. What a movie ends up grossing has nothing to do with the subject at hand. We are talking only about that first weekend. A star must deliver an eight-figure opening—that is, draw in a couple of million Americans in three days. That is his or her job.

One of the great bits of comedy available to us today concerns the failure of *Quiz Show*. It got great reviews and had great hype and died when it hit the boonies. "The timing of the release is what killed it—they should have gone wide faster and not treated it as an art film." Or, "The poster of that guy from behind turned people off." Or, "There were no stars in it, and quality movies only work if there are stars."

Hilarious stuff, that. Do you know who killed *Quiz Show*?

Quiz Show failed because of *you*—remember the old poster of Uncle Sam pointing?—*you* didn't like it. *You* didn't tell your friends. All hits are the result of only one thing: word of mouth.

Okay. Off we go. The following is from top studio agents, producers, and directors.

Usually, there is *a* biggest star. Two years ago: Schwarzenegger. But last year, for the first time, there were six stars tied for the lead. The six were Ford, Schwarzenegger, Gibson, Cruise, Costner, and Miss Julia. How firm is their footing now?

Harrison Ford (*Clear and Present Danger*): "As big as ever. No. Bigger." "I think he's the biggest star, but I'll tell you what's crazy—*he only does commercial films*. I know that's what stars are supposed to do, but lately he's only been doing the surefire stuff—sequels and big-screen-TV things. We don't really know with him. Will they follow him if he stretches? He hasn't taken a risk since *The Mosquito Coast*, and that was almost ten years ago. He was good, but it didn't work commercially."

Arnold Schwarzenegger (*True Lies* and *Junior*): "Right back where he was before *Last Action Hero*. A quarter-billion around the world." "I don't think he'd be worth much in *The Remains of the Day*, and please God, let's never find out, but worldwide, he may be the biggest again."

Mel Gibson (*Maverick*): "He has that charm, and any time he wants to use it, people just love him." "As big as anybody, and he takes more chances. Of course when he does, the pictures don't perform, but it hasn't hurt him."

Tom Cruise (*Interview With the Vampire*): "I think right now there is nothing they won't buy him in. Huge." "The trues test of a star is, How does he deliver in a stinker? Since he drew them in *Cocktail*, I've been a believer." "I detested the movie, and everyone I know who isn't a mouth breather detested that movie, and with anybody else in it—down the tubes.

But he's going to ride it to over $100 million, and no one is like him."

Julia Roberts (*I Love Trouble*): "After a flop like that, I don't put her in the top ten anymore. Remember something—that wasn't an art film, it was assembled for her; it was the kind of comedy/romance that shot her up there. And it tanked. That's why she's falling. If it had been a drama, no problem. But if this wasn't in her wheelhouse, what the hell is?" "She took a big hit—I think Demi Moore is bigger now."

Kevin Costner (*Wyatt Earp* and *The War*): "Burt Reynolds took years to lose it. Same with Eddie Murphy. I don't think it's remotely over." "I am sure his agents at CAA will tell you he's getting as many offers as before and his price is the same as before. And that may be true. But they're scared—my God, his next starring role is in *Waterworld*, and if that ends up being as big as *Jaws* it will *still* be a flop." "I am amazed at the turn his career's taken. I thought he would be up there for years. But he's sure not now." Personally, I cannot remember a star taking the hits Costner is at the moment. Everything has gone south, and we are reading all about it. *A Perfect World*, which disappointed, and in which he was wonderful, took in over $100 million foreign. But *Wyatt Earp* should have opened—his last Western, remember, was *Dances With Wolves*, which did okay. Now *The War* has aroused no interest. And jokes about *Waterworld*—it is currently being called *Underwater*—are making the rounds. So? I think he's going to be just fine. I think he's going to regroup and direct again and make us love him again.

Stay tuned.

It's clear that two of the six have definitely stumbled. And which of the big four is No. 1 this year? "Arnold." "Dead heat, Cruise and Ford." "Gibson and Cruise. No, Ford's up there with them. Did I say Arnold? Him too." A certain disagreement that needs to be settled.

The winner this year needs no envelope. Tom Hanks is the fellow. "*Amazing* what he's done—think about it—has anybody had four like this? *A League of Their Own* followed by *Sleepless in Seattle* followed by *Philadelphia* followed by *Forrest Gump*? Four huge hits, four hits of genuine quality, not to mention probably two Oscars? Never." "I'll tell you what makes Hanks even more incredible. Look at those four movies—they're famous now, but they sure as hell weren't, not when he signed on. They were *all* risky projects." "It's remarkable, but I think the public will follow him anywhere now."

My own feeling is that Hanks is something that hasn't happened since Bogart. He has *become* a great film actor before our eyes. Bogart in his first decade was ordinary. And then he changed. And as wonderful as Hanks was in *Splash*, who expected the breadth and depth of work he's turning out now?

So Hanks is the biggest acting star of '94, and hats off. Let's hope he continues to go his own way, ride clear of sequels, take the dares. He deserves everything he gets.

But one last thing—he is *not* the biggest star in movies. Who is? Mr. Spielberg, of course. No matter what his next movie turns out to be, if he directs it, we will come. For the first time in Hollywood history, a face that isn't even up on the screen is the face that most haunts our dreams.

—NOVEMBER 28, 1994

ANYTHING BUT GUMP

Among Hollywood machers, *it may be the most reviled best-loved movie ever. But come Oscar time, who'll have the chops to cut down 'Forrest'?*

In the event that Los Angeles manages to survive until February 14, there will be Academy Award nominations this year. What follows is an early report from the combat zone. Get ready—expect blood on the moon. And please remember two things: (1) The Oscars are *an industry award*, that industry being motion pictures, headquartered Out There. If the industry were automobiles and the city were Detroit, our Japanese peers would not fare well. (Nor should they.) (2) *There is no "best."* Tolstoy never won the Nobel Prize. Bach was ignored and unknown for a century after his death. And when movie critics give their ten-best lists, they may cite historical precedent, they may pretend erudition—all b.s. They just liked one movie better than another.

Often the Best Picture award is a one-on-one contest—*Schindler's List* vs. *The Piano*; *GoodFellas* vs. *Dances With Wolves*. Occasionally, three break on top and stay there: *Bonnie and Clyde* against *The Graduate* against *In the Heat of the Night*.

Sometimes four have a shot: *Chinatown*, *The Conversation*, *Godfather II*, and *Lenny* battled in 1974. And there is the occasional vintage year. How would you like to have picked from these five 1982 nominees: *E.T.* and *Gandhi* and *Missing* and *Tootsie* and *The Verdict*?

Nineteen ninety-five has no such Oscar abundance. But it has something at least as rare. Did people in Hollywood bitch about *It's a Wonderful Life*? Don't think so. Did Judy visiting Oz make people's teeth ache? Odds against. Who hated *Singin' in the Rain*? No hands raised.

But *Forrest Gump*, the dear front-runner and one of the greatest financial successes in history, is turning out to be the most loathed best-loved film ever.

The first indications came last August, when a studio executive going over the Christmas films, already suspected to be a weak bunch, said, "Look at this junk. Christ, *Forrest Gump* could win the Oscar." And then he paused before adding gratefully, "Thank God for *Quiz Show*."

Quiz Show had everything. A famous, Oscar-winning director, Robert Redford, at the peak of his form. Brilliant actors—Fiennes and Turturro and Scofield. But more than anything else, it was a Potential Oscar Winner because it dealt with issues dear to the hearts of the cultural elite, it was quote-unquote important, it described a moment when America lost its quote-unquote innocence.

And a fine film *Quiz Show* was. Splendid reviews, endless positive hype. And sadly, it died.

Ordinary people did not like it. And remember our first law: Disappointing box-office never makes a good industry standard-bearer. So scratch *Quiz Show* as a *Gump* killer. (Though it'll surely get many nominations.)

Two other hopefuls expired at the same time. *Ed Wood*,

Tim Burton's finest film yet, drew no one to whom he was not related into the theaters. And *The Shawshank Redemption*, with its off-putting title, went the way of *Quiz Show*, although it might still get nominations. For me, *Shawshank* was easily the dramatic movie of the year and featured the best male performance, by Morgan Freeman. He won't win. Nor will any of my other acting choices: Linda Fiorentino for *The Last Seduction* (actress)—which has been ruled ineligible in any case, because it first showed on HBO—Robin Wright for *Gump* (supporting actress); and Martin Landau for *Ed Wood* (supporting actor). Does that make me wrong? Check rule No. 2. There is no "best." It doesn't make me right either (though secretly I know I am).

Nell was the next Great White Hope. "I'm hearing really good things," one honcho said in early fall. "No one's seen it, but the word is great." Could it beat *Gump*? "Fingers crossed," came the reply.

After it opened, the honcho said this: "Loved her, hated it." Could it beat *Gump*? "It's got a better chance than *Love Affair*," was his glum response. Pause. Then, his voice brightening: "I'm hearing really good things about *Nobody's Fool*."

This time, the word was true. *Nobody's Fool* and *Little Women* became the best-reviewed movies of the holiday season. But were they dragon slayers? "Think about it: What is *Little Women*? The fifth remake of that material? When did the Academy ever vote for a remake? And *Nobody's Fool* is so small. I know *Marty* was small, and it won, but that was 40 years ago. I think they'll both get nominated and Ryder may win and Newman may win, but God—*Gump* is still up there."

Before we get to the final four contenders, it's time to talk to some *Gump* haters and try to understand their passion.

"Frankly, I hate it because it is such a huge hit," says the first. "If it had done $30 million at the box, I would have been mildly dyspeptic. If it had done $5 million, I would have beamed. But it did *$300 million*, and I hate all movies that do that kind of business—because I've never had one."

Said a second honcho, "Of course envy is involved. But that's too easy. Look—this year the media have been all over us because of what they perceive as lack of quality. They claim we're making stupid, mindless movies. And here comes *Forrest Gump*, which *glorifies* stupidity."

The third highly placed insider nailed it. "Look at its most famous line. The truth is that if you open a box of chocolates, you know *exactly* what you're going to get. Ask anybody at Russell Stover. No question *Gump* is a brilliant piece of filmmaking. But the fact is, the country is getting dumber, and this movie celebrates that. Don't you get it, Goldman? We are in the movie business, and *this movie does not serve us well!*"

The first of the four movies that remain to be considered is *The Lion King*. Its strength is simply this: It may end up the most commercially successful film ever. Weakness: "It's an animated film. You think *actors* are going to vote for a fucking *drawing?* Next case."

Four Weddings and a Funeral. Many strengths: great reviews, great word of mouth, fresh, different, the most brilliant screenplay of the year (by Richard Curtis), the explosion of Hugh Grant, a surprise hit in America, a phenomenon in the rest of the world. Weakness: "It's a comedy. That kills it. You know and I know comedy is much harder to pull off than drama, but the Academy doesn't see it that way. I think *Annie Hall* was the last comedy winner, and that was in the seventies."

Pulp Fiction. Strengths: Let's put it this way—try to find a weakness. It won at Cannes. It killed them at the New York Film Festival. It has done wonderful business. (If *Quiz Show* had been as successful, it would have been the favorite.) It has put John Travolta back on top, and the Academy loves comebacks. It has a remarkable performance by Samuel L. Jackson that could win in either acting category. It has a remarkable screenplay by Quentin Tarantino. It has wonderful direction by Quentin Tarantino. It has the critics scrambling to find new and even more fabulously glorious adjectives.

And . . . and . . . and—it has a creation myth worthy of *Forrest Gump*.

Because as everyone knows, *Forrest Gump* is your standard Hollywood extravaganza, a megastar vehicle for Tom Hanks beloved and embraced by all the major studios, while *Pulp Fiction* is an art-house flower that somehow, with pluck and luck, fought through the cracks in the sidewalk and saw the sky. A most unusual David, if you will, fighting your ho-hum Goliath.

Like many myths, this one has a loose connection to reality.

Winston Groom's novel *Forrest Gump* was published and optioned for films in 1985, and the movie was released in 1994. They didn't wait nine years because they *wanted* to. The fact is, nobody much understood the notion of history as viewed by a sweet idiot savant—too uncommercial. Screenplays were written and discarded. The picture was put in turnaround by one studio and picked up by Paramount. It wasn't until 1992 that Eric Roth delivered the script that finally galvanized the project and for which he will win the Oscar, the one lock, say I, in the entire event. So, *Forrest Gump* has been unbeloved for about a decade.

But people sure dug *Pulp Fiction*—the script was optioned *before* it was even written. The excellence of Tarantino's earlier *Reservoir Dogs* was enough to attract top producers. The only reason Miramax, a leading distributor of art films, got it was that TriStar, which has been undergoing some kind of a cold streak, had it, read it, and turned it down. And Tarantino, who may know more about movies than anybody, wanted to do a commercial film for his second directing effort.

Doesn't *Pulp Fiction* have any Achilles heel? Sure. The age of the Academy members. "When I go to an Academy screening," explained one power, "I always feel like I'm the youngest one there, and I'm 60. And of course, *Pulp Fiction* is very violent, which they don't ordinarily like. But when the nominations come out, if it does better than expected, then maybe the voters are trying to be 'with it' this year. And if that happens, it might win. But I think most of us will be shocked if *Gump* doesn't take it. The reality is, it should, when you take everything into consideration. I'm betting that it will—but last year, I bet on *The Piano*." (Last year, of course, *Schindler's List* won Best Picture.)

My own feelings? I agree with one leading agent who explained, "*Dumb and Dumber* is a stupid movie about stupid people. *Forrest Gump* is a very smart movie. And it isn't about dumbness at all. It's a Capra film—it's about *innocence*. I wish more people were willing to see it that way."

I sat through *Pulp Fiction* and *Forrest Gump* knowing nothing in advance about either film, and I found them wonderfully similar: They took me to places where I hadn't been and I hadn't expected to go. Cheers to them both.

Now for the fourth movie that needs mentioning: *Hoop Dreams*. If it wins (and it won't), Newt Gingrich will not be happy. But for me, it's the movie experience of the decade. Of course, we're only halfway through. And being movie fans, we are all desperate optimists. Miracles may lie in store these next five years. Wonders may unfold before us. Who knows, if we live long enough, Jim Carrey could even have a hit.

—JANUARY 30, 1995

What Should Win Best Picture?

Hint: It's not 'Quiz Show,' 'Pulp Fiction,' 'Forrest Gump,' or 'Four Weddings and a Funeral'

Oscar nominations are out and the tea leaf readers are busy indeed. But this year, not many shockers. Oh, sure, a few. How did *Four Weddings and a Funeral* get a Best Picture nomination and Hugh Grant not get a Best Actor bid? It wasn't as if he had this teeny-weeny-itty-bitty scene—hell, the guy's in every frame. And can you name another actor in the world who would have helped the movie more? I sure can't. And the Academy's embrace of Woody Allen—no one foresaw that. *Bullets Over Broadway* was going to get nominations, but seven? Including Best Director? Newt will glom on to this as further proof that Hollywood is an even greater threat to World Survival than overpopulation. And most inexplicable and sad— *Hoop Dreams* being ignored.

But all the gnashing in the world is standard and meaningless—what matters about the nominations is the same as what's important about the awards themselves: the insight they give as to the taste of the industry *at a particular point in time*. Remember—I know you know this but I have to say it anyway—there is no right or wrong choice here. It is not mathematics. When I say I think *Schindler's List* is a greater artistic achievement than *The Piano*, all I am really saying is that I liked it more.

The media have been all over Hollywood this year for the low quality of movies, and, frankly, I don't get it. For me, the year has been easily the best of the decade, not so much in that there have been masterpieces but in that there have been so many terrific flicks. And the five nominated Best Pictures truly deserve to be there.

Quiz Show. When Robert Redford is dealing with his favorite theme, fraudulence, he is as good as the game. Wonderful acting—how did John Turturro not get nominated?—and a million other pluses.

But I didn't get all that involved, and I think I can tell you why—the movie could not go deeply into the dynamics of the Van Doren family. Because it did not have the cooperation of the Van Doren family. And that hurt. How about a scene in which the mother and the son face each other for the first time after his "sin" has been exposed to the world? How about a scene in which the father and the mother talk with Charley about not ever having seen him, their beloved son, on TV? Think about that in your own life: Your mother or father or husband or wife or child suddenly becomes the most famous face in America, not for being a murderer but for being brilliant, and you don't watch? *Not even once?* If that's a loving family, I don't want to see them when they're peeved with each other. For me the movie did wonderfully with what it had. It's what it didn't have that bothered me.

Forrest Gump and *Pulp Fiction.* I liked them both a lot and I liked them both the same. For me, in some nutty way, they were the same movie. Wonderful, unusual stories going wonderful, unexpected places. Award-caliber acting—how did

Robin Wright not get nominated?—and a million other pluses.

But I thought that they were both way too long. I was really bored by the sequence in *Forrest Gump* in which Gump—for no reason whatsoever except to explain how some time has passed—jogs around what seems to be the entire civilized world for what seems to be hours. What *was* that? Coming near the end, it was damaging.

And what was that sequence in *Pulp Fiction* with Harvey Keitel? We're in two hours and this bloody body is in the car and this *genius* is called in to save the situation and what does he say? Something like: "Okay, guys, cover up the blood with blankets, you're saved, see ya." That's genius? And I guess no movie can win Best Picture if it requires John Travolta to have bowel trouble in order for the plot to work.

Probably what I'm saying is that, for me, neither film accumulated.

Four Weddings and a Funeral. The hardest movie of the year to pull off. And I think if Audrey Hepburn could have played the girl, I wouldn't have been the only one voting it Best Picture. But Andie MacDowell—who was lovely and very likely the reason the picture got made—is not a fanciful performer. And here you wanted a girl who could fly. The only scene that doesn't work in the whole flick is the final love scene in the rain. It just wasn't magical. I left the theater not with thoughts of love and everlasting happiness but rather wondering how long these two would stay together.

I am voting for **The Shawshank Redemption** because—and I am speaking here as an intellectual writing for an intellectual magazine—*it moved the shit out of me.*

Yes, it was too long, but I could not figure out where to cut it. (Maybe the James Whitmore part.) But that's my one gripe.

It took me places I hadn't been and hadn't expected to go. It accumulated. And Morgan Freeman was so moving and so real.

And so still.

The hardest thing for an actor is to be still. Just stand there and let the magic happen behind your eyes. There is a belief loose in the land that what's hard is playing the lame, the halt, and the blind. Wrong. Actors *kill* for those parts. A reason to overact? Heaven.

Anyway, that's my Best Picture vote. I'm not saying I'm right. There is no right. There is only what moves you. I know someone in the movie business who thinks the greatest film of all time is *Pretty in Pink*. Isn't that just amazingly stupid? I mean, I thought everybody knew it was *Gunga Din*.

—APRIL 1995

THE FOLLOWING WERE ACADEMY AWARD WINNERS FOR 1994:

Best Actor	*Tom Hanks, Forrest Gump*
Best Actress	*Jessica Lange, Blue Sky*
Best Director	*Robert Zemeckis, Forrest Gump*
Best Picture	*Forrest Gump*

OSCAR DEMOCRACY

Okay, the Academy Awards are what they are. But they'd actually be interesting—even useful—if we knew how the industry voted.

Red wine is, almost by definition, great. Still, you wouldn't want to hock the farm for a '92 Bordeaux. So it was with this year's Oscars—great, yes, of course; they're always that. But not one for the time capsule.

Before it began, some 100-most-powerful types were braced for disaster. "It will be worse than the Chinese water torture—it will be nothing but *Gump*, *Gump*, *Gump*, till you go mad." This from a famous director. Said an agent of renown: "It will be the most predictable awards show ever—the only surprise would be if there was a surprise."

And afterward? I'll spare you their quotes. Just know this: They didn't like it much. But one of them added something helpful: "Next year, they've got to make it better or they've got to make it worse." We'll come back to that in a moment.

But first, let's go after Sharon Stone. As much as anybody, Sharon Stone sums up what was wrong with the Oscars

'95. What was she thinking, being seen in public looking like that? She is the sex symbol of our time, and here she was, a billion people watching, and she was *elegant*. I can forgive her being beautiful—she is beautiful—but does she have to be sophisticated too? Has the woman no sense of shamelessness? Where were her advisers? Anna Nicole Smith would never betray us like that.

So, the problem with this year's Oscars? Waaaaaay too tasteful.

Where was Cher when we needed her? Where was Richard Gere? Sally Field had center stage, and not once did she get emotional. Susan and Tim, as glamorous and gifted a couple as we have (now that Julia and Lyle have broken my heart); totally let me down. I want my overwrought self-righteous pleas for the homeless. How else am I supposed to know if the Dalai Lama is still okay?

A few personal kudos.

Greatest acting performance: Tom Hanks during the spinning-dog pet trick. Pale, a sickly smile, his hands clasped over his crotch. I have never seen a star of any magnitude show such terror. In one minute, he obliterated all my memories of Janet Leigh in the shower.

Greatest suck-up job: Martin Landau. He thanked a critic.

Greatest acceptance speeches: the writer, star, director, and three producers of *Forrest Gump*. Not one of them found it in their hearts to utter the words *Winston* and *Groom* in succession. It's obviously a well-kept secret, but author Winston Groom did write the novel that made them all even richer.

Greatest standing ovation: for Michelangelo Antonioni. You probably didn't know the fervor for this guy that exists in Southern California. There are studio heads who can give you

Zabriskie Point shot for shot. One of the intellectual high points of my life was when I was invited to the famous Bel Air Nihilism Society, which meets on Thursdays, and heard a discussion of water images in *La Notte*. Anyway, it's nice to see that passion made public.

Worst omission: not one Kato joke. What is that? The guy's an actor, a fellow union member, and he's treated as if he never existed. Do you realize what the great Johnny Carson would have done with the idea of Judge Ito's worrying that the Oscar telecast might somehow influence the poor-bastard jury?

But enough of honors. It's time to get back to the suggestion about making the show better or worse. *Worse* does not exist in my lexicon. The Oscars are what they are, and everybody who criticizes them for being tacky just doesn't get it. But we can make them better. Here's how:

What would you think if, on November 12, 1996, the speaker of the House stood in front of a battery of TV cameras and said this: "The president is now Bob Dole. Good night"?

Insane, yes? Would any of us stand for it? No. Would anyone defend such a system? Not likely.

It is time for the Academy to let us know how its members voted.

Think a minute. This year, the wisdom was that the race was between *Forrest Gump* and *Pulp Fiction*—but we can't be sure. All I know is this: I have met few human beings who liked *Pulp Fiction* as much as the critics did. But I know a lot of people who liked *The Shawshank Redemption* more than most of our opinion-makers. Maybe *Shawshank* was second. Maybe *Pulp Fiction* damn near won it all. Why don't we possess this information?

We ought to be able to accurately sense the mood of the industry, just as in elections we can sense the mood of the country. Of course the Oscars are a publicity stunt, but they have become, over almost 70 years, more than that. They've become the lead phrase in our obits.

—APRIL 10, 1995

THE NIGHTMARE BEFORE CHRISTMAS

Do you care about the upcoming Christmas pictures? I hope you do. I used to. I don't now. Not this year. *Entertainment Weekly*, *Time*, and the *Time Magazine* all ran recent major articles to the effect that TV was better than movies. And you know what? They're right. At least they're right this year.

I think in the period from January through October 1995, Hollywood has brought us comedies so unfunny, action so uninterestingly blood-spattered, rapes so unending, movies so inexcusably stupid, degrading, and awful, that it's fair to say this: We have just lived through the worst ten months in the history of sound.

Last year at this time, *The Shawshank Redemption* had opened. *Quiz Show* had opened. And *Forrest Gump*. And *Pulp Fiction*.

If the Oscars were held over just the first ten months of this year, there would be one lock Best Picture nomination— *Apollo 13*. A terrific picture, I thought. Solid, professional movie-making. But solid, professional moviemaking should be the norm, not what wins awards. The only "best picture" of the first ten months, for me, was *Babe*. It was the one time I felt a genuine imagination at work. But *Babe*, alas, has nothing to do with what's going on in Southern California.

And what's going on in Southern California is best summed up in the Universal Pictures-Sylvester Stallone deal. The published information was simply this: Universal was to pay the actor $60 million for three as-yet-unspecified films.

Three movies. Maybe 30 weeks' work. Sixty million. Biggest star deal ever.

There was a certain amount of criticism from the media when the announcement came—concerning the amount. But Universal should not be criticized; lots of studios would have leapt at the arrangement. Universal, perhaps because it had been taken over by the man who was, until a few weeks earlier, Stallone's agent, just got there first. And Stallone would have been dumb—which he is not; he is very, very smart—if he hadn't accepted. Whatever Sylvester Stallone earns is his private affair. It's wrong for anybody to find fault with the finances.

One can, however, pause a moment over the message that the deal sent around the world. And here is what Universal, and by implication all Hollywood, is saying: *Hey, everybody, listen, we've got great news: We're gonna make more shit.*

These are the movies Sylvester Stallone has chosen to star in over the past ten years: *Assassins*; *Judge Dredd*; *The Specialist*; *Demolition Man*; *Cliffhanger*; *Stop! Or My Mom Will Shoot*; *Oscar*; *Rocky V*; *Tango & Cash*; *Lock Up*; *Rambo III*; *Over the Top*; *Cobra*.

What to say? Well, there isn't going to be any *Stop! Or My Mom Will Shoot Again.* And to my knowledge, no studio is readying *Tango & Cash II.* Does anyone love or cherish any of them? Or even think of them fondly? Do you remember in the wonderful Jimmy Cagney comedy *One Two Three* when the communists tortured Horst Buchholz by playing "Itsy Bitsy

Teenie Weeny Yellow Polka Dot Bikini" until he did what they wanted? How long do you think you'd hold if you had those thirteen movies played over and over for you in a locked room? Under these conditions, there is nothing I wouldn't admit to.

If this is taken as a criticism of Stallone, it's not meant to be. He is one of the biggest stars in history, and he is, like all stars, trapped within his persona. Robin Williams does comedy; when he leaves his genre—anybody see *Being Human?*— the public tends not to respond. Can we criticize Williams for staying primarily with comedy? Nope.

Stallone has tried escaping, but his public did not respond. So he did what stars have always done and will always do—they try to remain stars. Because the fall is too painful. I may not have liked any of the pictures on the list, but who knows how dreadful the stuff he turned down was? Stallone has done what he does best: mindless violence. And though his audience has been diminishing in America, he is still gigantic in Taiwan.

What the sum of $60 million, and the announcement of this sum, was saying was this: It's okay to kill as many people as you want. Kill without conscience. Kill without consequence. Kill with only one proviso: There must be pretty blood.

Hollywood, right now, is like baseball: arrogant and, because of that arrogance, in genuine trouble. Baseball thinks the fans will come back, because they always have. And that's true—so far, the fans always have. But that was in a different world. Before 76-channel cable TV and computers and CD-ROMs and cheap air travel. There wasn't that much to do with leisure time in the old days.

Hollywood thinks that if they make it, you will come. And you always have. But if the Stallone deal is a touchstone, change is very much in the air. They are not bothering to make movies for you anymore. They figure you have nowhere else to go.   So Hollywood has decided to make movies for mouth breathers in Southeast Asia.

And if they continue on their present path, we may look back on these ten months nostalgically: A few years down the line, we may all be longing for *Showgirls*.

To end on an upbeat note, my first Oscar prediction: Emma Thompson will he the first woman ever nominated for Best Actress and Best Screenplay in the same year, for *Sense and Sensibility*. Yours in torment . . .

—NOVEMBER 20, 1995

APOCALYPSE NOW

That 1995 was a horrid year for movies augurs very badly indeed for the future of the industry. But how about that Jim Carrey?

Hollywood is headed straight off a cliff; the crash will occur in the next eighteen months, and very painful it will be— like sitting through *Four Rooms* twice. But before we get to the carnage, let's turn to a sexier subject (and a not unconnected one), that being our annual discussion of this most important of all questions: Who is the biggest star in the world?

Three years ago, it was Arnold. Because not only had his previous four movies, *Terminator 2* among them, taken in more than a billion dollars at box-offices worldwide—all four had also *opened*. (Please remember that as far as the studios are concerned, a star is responsible not for what a movie ultimately grosses, or even what it costs, but for how it draws that first, crucial, opening weekend.)

A half-step behind Schwarzenegger came Kevin Costner. Also with four straight hits, among them *Dances With Wolves*.

And then three in a dead heat: Mr. Cruise, Mr. Gibson, and Miss Roberts.

The next year found *six* in a dead heat, Schwarzenegger and Costner having taken small hits that brought them back to the pack. The reigning six were—billing alphabetically, of course—Arnold, Harrison, Julia, Kevin, Mel, and Tom C.

Last year, Costner fell out of it with *Wyatt Earp* and *The War*, and Julia Roberts was damaged by *I Love Trouble*, leaving the other four—Cruise and Ford and Gibson and Schwarzenegger—tied.

Tied for third, that is.

Tom Hanks had rocketed past them and was now the biggest star in the world—the biggest *acting* star. Because Steven Spielberg sat on the throne, uncontested, the biggest star of all—the first time ever for a nonperformer.

This year, a really remarkable changing of the guard.

Cruise didn't have a picture.

Harrison Ford: "Of course *Sabrina* hurt him." This from a *Premiere* 100 Hollywood-power-broker type. "It didn't open. Put him in a Clancy, *Indiana Jones*, one of those—he's as big as ever. The guy's good for years—but no more romance. Action is where it is for him now."

To my mind, *Sabrina* is the curio of the year. Whose horrible idea was it to do it again? All that talent toiling for what?—it could never touch the original. As far as I'm concerned, you only remake *Sabrina* if Julia Ormond played it the first time and Audrey Hepburn suddenly happened.

Mel Gibson? The *Premiere* 100 guy again: "A great year for him as an artist, a good year only as a commercial star. *Braveheart* sets him up as a major director—I think he may get a nomination for it, and I think he should—but it cost a fortune and didn't make one. Everyone was saying 'at least a hundred million at the box,' and what did it do, two thirds of that? He's starting into what will be a major career, but I don't think anyone would put him at the very top of the list; soon, maybe, just not this year."

Schwarzenegger was wonderful, I thought, in *Junior*, but his public wasn't there. Said an agent who would kill to have him, "I think he'll have hits in the future, sure, but only violence films. A few years ago we thought his fans would follow him anywhere—comedy, you name it—but now it's clear they won't. He's just another blood star."

Spielberg is out of it for the present—hasn't screamed "Cut!" for very nearly three years. A waste of a prodigious and important talent, but maybe not unexpected. A friend of his said this when *Schindler's List* came out: "If he wins, I think it will rock him. All his life he's wanted to be accepted, and God knows, that's happened. But be careful what you wish for; you might get it. I think he's going to win and I want that for him, but I wouldn't be surprised if it was years before he worked again."

Leaving Tom Hanks. He was the biggest acting star last year, and he continued a genuinely phenomenal streak. Five movies in four years. And here they are:

A League of Their Own

Sleepless in Seattle

Philadelphia

Forrest Gump

Apollo 13

Twenty nominations, with a bunch more to come this year. Two consecutive Best Actor awards, with another nomination to come this year. Five critical and commercial successes. So if he was the biggest acting star last year, when you throw in *Apollo 13*, doesn't he have to be the biggest acting star this year? Sorry, Charlie.

There may never before have been anything like Jim Carrey. Certainly not since *Jaws* changed everything by ushering in the "blockbuster" era, which is still, alas, very much with us.

Like Hanks, Carrey has had five consecutive hits. But Hanks has worked with famous directors, famous co-stars. Excluding *Batman Forever*, Carrey's been out there alone. Can you think of anybody he's worked with who's been nominated for anything? And Hanks gets great notices, which he deserves.

Carrey does, too—who else can do what he can?—but for now, it's easier to take potshots at him. (Three pictures down the line, when he does *The Truman Show* directed by Peter Weir, that's all going to change.)

Oh, yes—almost forgot—most amazing of all, Carrey's done all this *in eighteen months*. "It's not supposed to be like that," said a studio minion. "One movie a year is supposed to be tops. You make one and sell the shit out of it, and then the next year you make another and sell that. Jim Carrey has broken every rule, and all that happens is he gets more popular. It's a freak thing. Can't last forever."

Only agents last forever, but right now, if you want Jim Carrey to make you rich, you will have to fork over $20 million, that being the price Columbia paid him for *Cable Guy*. "Those assholes," a competitive studio fellow said. "They ruined it. Do you know what they did?—at least what I hear they did? They flat-out offered him the money—no negotiations—just 'Here, please take it.' Once that happened, then everybody started getting twenty. It's insanity. Where in hell does it end?"

It ends this year, when somebody gets $25 million for a flick. And then every male name mentioned so far will demand

and receive $25 million for a flick.

And then—straight off a cliff.

None of this is meant to blame the actors. Nor is it meant to indicate that what's ahead is because of their deals. But the movie business has crashed twice in the past 30 years— late sixties, early eighties—and each time, the cry has been the same: "Those goddamned greedy actors are ruining us!"

No single element is destroying movies. Historically, Hollywood has never been as fiscally sound as widgetmaking. But events are happening now that simply have never happened before.

The Japanese caused a lot of it when they took over Sony and paid a ton to get Peter Guber and Jon Peters, successful producers, to run things. Being a studio head used to be a lousy job—terrible pressure and not that much money, and humiliation when you got canned.

Now it's a great job. Private jets and unlimited spending and huuuge salaries. And, and, and it's *wonderful* when you fail.

Peters left Sony early on; Guber stayed until they ripped off his epaulets. Sony took a write-off of more than $2.5 billion. Making Guber one of the least successful movie executives of all time.

But wait—do not think Fox or the Brothers Warner also lost money during that same period; these were golden times. Guber managed to piss away $2.5 billion while other studios were earning amazing amounts of money. Making Guber not just one of the least successful movie executives of all time but one of the least successful business executives of all time—*and he was rewarded*.

When Sony finally changed administrations, it gave

Guber arguably the best deal of any producer's in history. He's still with the company, and it gave him the keys to the vault. An agent familiar with the negotiation called it "astonishing, unprecedented."

But Guber is in the business of entertainment, not entertainment itself. So let's touch on a recent holiday movie: *Cutthroat Island*. No one doubts it will eventually lose $100 million—Geena Davis and her husband, director Renny Harlin, have managed to bust a company (Carolco) and put their thumbprints on arguably the biggest stiff in American movie history.

And they are rewarded.

At the moment, they are working together again on a script by Shane Black, the hottest young screenwriter going, and—I'll bet the farm on this—they both got raises.

Put it in a sports context: Make Peter Guber the coach of the Giants. If he managed to lose, say, 32 consecutive games, as well as bankrupt the franchise, his life would not be safe on the sidewalks of New York. In Hollywood, they make him commissioner of the league.

Okay, why give him that contract?

Well, among other things, the studios are making too many movies. As a producer, Peter Guber was a major player—*Batman*, *Rain Man*, etc. Since Sony is financing all these movies, someone has to produce them. And I'm sure that if Sony hadn't grabbed him, there was a long line for his services. And Renny Harlin directed *Cliffhanger*. And Geena Davis starred in *A League of Their Own*. Someone has to direct this stuff, someone has to star.

So why are they making too many movies?

No single reason. Part of it is the belief—and there is

merit here—that revenue from Europe and Asia will save them. And part of it has to do with the notion of market share. Buena Vista (Disney) won this year—19 percent—and even if you don't particularly care about that, you'd better believe it's a very big deal Out There.

But I think most of the overproduction is because of that ever-loving Hollywood pastime: dick swinging. "If that bastard's going to make twenty movies a year, I'm going to make twenty movies a year."

And what's wrong with making too many movies?

Well, among other things, there's this weeny problem—it's financially disastrous. Yes, *Babe*, before it's done, with the toys and the sequels, will make tens of millions, and *Toy Story* will make ten times that. But as one studio person who had a good year this year said, "Believe me, no one had a good year this year."

Look, let's say the gods demand we put out a movie a month. Well, one of the first things we have to do is this: Make our movie stand out. If six or ten movies are heading in next Friday, we must cut ourselves away from the herd.

How?

Easiest solution: Hire a star.

But, but, but—there aren't enough of them.

So we'll give them more money.

They're worth it, right?

Well, the media would not stop salivating over John Travolta after *Get Shorty* became a hit. Maniac articles. *He wants 21 mil for his next job. And he's worth it, right?*

Why did no one but primarily friends and relatives attend *White Man's Burden*? Because I have been a fan of John

Travolta's since he exploded in *Saturday Night Fever*—but I don't want to see him act, for Chrissakes. I don't want to see him suffer. I want him to be John Travolta.

The picture is the star.

The picture is always the star. Has always been.

Hard to believe, I know. True, though.

It's not actors alone. Top directors are now up to seven million per and heading for ten. Screenwriters for hire are closing in on two (though, personally, I must take this opportunity to complain that I have always been egregiously underpaid). Composers won't sniff at a quarter of a million.

The average Hollywood release is now $50 million—that's the cost of producing the film itself, plus prints and advertising. "I think that may be low now," said a young lady producer. "Maybe very low." Let's stay with $50 million. Of course, that's a scary number. But what's really scary is this: not how much flops lose but how relatively little most successes make.

In the late sixties, Hollywood was paying the Burtons a million each (a mere $4.4 million today, with inflation) to star in stiffs like *Boom!* A little more than a decade later, we had *Heaven's Gate* and *Raise the Titanic!*

Here we are again.

What's going to happen? Same old crap. Stars will be vilified. Executives will be fired. Fewer movies (I hope) will get green-lighted. The choices for those few movies will be even more timid (I hope not). Independent films will be hurt by the chilly financial climate.

And of course it's happened before, but I'm not sure of a happy ending this time. Because there are so many alternative things to do—television has gotten shockingly better and computers aren't going away. Have you bought a CD-ROM yet? You will. And your first won't be your last.

Plus, most important, this: The quality of what Hollywood is turning out is so foul, people are beginning to turn away. Attendance was flat this year—and what if that's a beginning? (Remember when the three major TV networks had more than 90 percent of the total viewing audience? That percentage is in the fifties now.) Broadway has been laughed at for years for not having enough quality stuff to nominate for the Tonys. Well, Oscar time is coming up.

Welcome to the theater.

One of the most important people in the industry said this: "You are wrong when you say we're going off a cliff— we've already gone over. We're in free fall now."

But as always, there's a bright side: Want to hear something really smart? They're doing another *Titanic* movie. Shooting mostly underwater. Going to cost at least a hundred million. I don't know about you, but I've already got my popcorn.

—JANUARY 22, 1996

THE PIG AND THE HUNK

*The surprisingly masterly 'Babe' and the surprisingly talented direc-
tor Mel Gibson are only two of the many surprises of this strange
Oscar season.*

The Academy Award nominations—this is being written the night before the announcements—figure to be the most
unpredictable, and therefore the most interesting, we've had in
a very long time. Because there are no favorites. No movie has
the industry in its thrall, as *Forrest Gump* did last year.

For me, there is only one lock, in the sense that
Schindler's List was a lock for a Best Picture nomination or
Anthony Hopkins for a Best Actor nomination in *The Silence of
the Lambs*, and that one certainty is Emma Thompson for Best
Screenplay adaptation, for *Sense and Sensibility*.

After her, the deluge.

Example—here are nine conceivable Best Actress fa-
vorites: Bening (*An American President*), Berry (*Losing Isaiah*),
Kidman (*To Die For*), Leigh (*Georgia*), Sarandon (*Dead Man
Walking*), Shue (*Leaving Las Vegas*), Stone (*Casino*), Streep (*The
Bridges of Madison County*), Thompson.   All have either won

some kind of official kudo this year or come close to winning some kind of official kudo this year or been touted as potential winners by one of the sports books in Vegas.

(Bally's in late December, for example, had Halle Berry rated third, behind Meryl Streep, who was even money, and Elisabeth Shue, at 2-1.)

For me—and I am totally biased since I was involved with the film—no one gave a better performance than Kathy Bates in *Dolores Claiborne*.

Will Bates get remembered? A female *Premiere* 100-type executive said this: "It didn't do enough business. Same with Leigh in *Georgia*. But then, neither did *Blue Sky*, and that didn't stop Jessica Lange from winning last year. This category is the most painful for me—so many years we don't have nearly enough women's work that deserves nominating, and this year, just too much."

A top agent said this: "I can give you a scenario where *Dead Man Walking* gets half a dozen nominations, and another where it gets shut out. I can see *Bridges of Madison County* the same way. And I can absolutely see that with *Leaving Las Vegas* and *Braveheart*. Goldman, have you told your readers about the *age* of the Academy members?"

Good point. Try "ancient."

Probably overdoing it. But there are few tykes.

And you know something? If there were a preponderance of very young voters, none of the movies mentioned so far would get a Best Picture nomination. Because this has been a remarkable year for children's pictures. And no, not one of them is *Pocahontas*:

A Little Princess

Babe

The Indian in the Cupboard

The Secret of Roan Inish (just a wonderful film)

Toy Story

On the mention of *Toy Story*, a studio guy exploded—
"Time out. Why doesn't that get nominated for everything it
could possibly be up for? Look at it logically—the biggest
commercial hit and the best-reviewed flick. Isn't that what's
supposed to win out here? Call me after the announcements,
and I'll explain it all to you then."

The Academy Award nominations—this is being written the afternoon after the announcements were made—have
turned out to be so bewildering that everyone is in a state of
shock Out There. No one is explaining anything. Here is what
my wizards had to say about the way the Academy voted: nothing.

A bewildered silence from one and all. Eventually followed by low moans.

"It's not possible that I can be so confused," said one
softly. "Don't ask me anything, I don't know anything," replied
a peer. From a third, this: "Call me later. I'm still in shock."
There were no trends spotted. No logic apparent. The only
point anyone would talk to was which nomination or omission
most rocked him—the lack of recognition for John Travolta
and Ron Howard being the complaint heard most frequently.

But having nothing to report has never stopped any
journalist from reporting, so I thought I would write about
what I'm going to vote for in the only two categories I'm sure
of at this moment, Best Picture and Best Director. (And please
remember, when I say what I think is best, I simply mean what
I liked the most.)

The Best Picture nominees are

Apollo 13

Babe

Braveheart

The Postman (Il Postino)

Sense and Sensibility

Let me get rid of *The Postman* first: I thought it was slow—yes, I understand that European films have a different style of storytelling—and boring. And my final thought was that the male star, Massimo Troisi, was responsible for much of the reaction of the Academy—not just because he was so splendid and touching in the title role but because he died the day after the picture finished shooting. A terrible thing for his family, but it made for a great and poignant media story. I won't go into the details here; I promise you'll be sick of them come March 25.

Harder to dismiss are *Apollo 13* and *Sense and Sensibility*. I liked them both enormously, and listed them both in my nomination ballot for Best Picture. In a strange way, I also thought they were the same picture: solid, intelligent, sturdy moviemaking. I wish we had twenty like them each year. (We did, once—you have to go back a very long time for that.) But I did not think *Sense and Sensibility* was really much better than several recent Merchant Ivory movies. (Which I also did not vote for.) And as for *Apollo 13*, the blastoff sequence was thrilling; the floating, neat; the acting, fine. If it wins, I'll be happy. But it doesn't get my vote.

Braveheart doesn't, either. Though if it had ended after two hours or thereabouts, it would have. But in the last hour, director Mel Gibson allowed the story to shift: A movie that had been about a man—Gibson's character, William Wallace—

became a movie about a cause, Scottish freedom. I did not buy the shift, was confused by it, and found the last third a different movie, and one I did not like all that much.

I loved all of *Babe*. It was inventive from the start, original from the start—it didn't remind me of any other movie. And it had my year's favorite character moment—when the farmer dances. (My favorite acting moment is in *Sense and Sensibility* when Emma Thompson bursts into tears.)

So *Babe* gets my vote. In an ordinary year, maybe not. But in this dreadful twelve months of bloodbaths and low I.Q. comedy, hats off.

Now to the Best Director nominees:

Chris Noonan for *Babe*

Mel Gibson for *Braveheart*

Tim Robbins for *Dead Man Walking*

Mike Figgis for *Leaving Las Vegas*

Michael Radford for *The Postman*

The Postman is again the first to go. For me, ordinary work. (But it's a genuine triumph for a foreign-language film to do this well. And a remarkable success for the Miramax advertising and publicity people. They had faith, kept plugging away, and they did it.) And again, let me lump two of them together: *Dead Man Walking* and *Leaving Las Vegas*. Terrific stuff from both Tim Robbins and Mike Figgis. Two movies these two unusual talents desperately wanted to make. And somehow got them done. And I think one or the other will get the award. And whatever their next movies are, they won't be as hard to get done as these two babies must have been. They deserve everything they're both going to get.

So does Chris Noonan, who directed my pick for Best

Picture. I can't wait for his next movie. But as wonderful as *Babe* was, it was the concept that soared the highest for me.

Mel Gibson gets my vote for *Braveheart*. Why? Because even though I find fault with some of the storytelling, the execution of the film was simply phenomenal. The battle sequences were dazzling, the sense of time and place and pain beautifully delivered.

There is a myth, mostly propagated by directors, that the best picture has to also be the best-directed picture.

B.S., said he, daintily.

Five weeks till the Big Event. By then the Monday-morning quarterbacks will have recovered, regrouped, explained what the nominations meant and who the Oscar winners will be. Believe nothing.

—FEBRUARY 26, 1996

THE FOLLOWING WERE ACADEMY AWARD WINNERS FOR 1995:

Best Actor	*Nicolas Cage, Leaving las Vegas*
Best Actress	*Susan Sarandon, Dead Man Walking*
Best Director	*Mel Gibson, Braveheart*
Best Picture	*Braveheart*

STAY ANGRY

*ASIDE FROM SOME MOVING MOMENTS (KIRK, CHRISTOPHER) AND
AMUSING INTERLUDES (SHARON, EMMA) THE OSCARS WERE AS
INFURIATING AS HOLLYWOOD ITSELF.*

When this century's culture is put in the time capsule,
what are the locks? Something by Hopper, absolutely. *The
Prodigal Son* by Balanchine, a must. No question about *Porgy
and Bess*. Radio: Orson's vision of the Martians invading. For
movies, obviously, *Gunga Din.*

What about television, though? Eggheads might go for
Joe Welch at last bringing down McCarthy. Dramaturgs could
head toward *Marty*. But I'm sorry, nothing, *nothing* displays
America's sheer greatness of soul as much as the Academy
Awards.

As I worked myself into shape for this year's version, I
think I was most grateful to the Academy for *not* nominating
Ron Howard for Best Director. All he did was bring home one
of the two or three best-reviewed *and* most commercial films
eligible. You think it was *easy* having those three schmucks sar-
dined in a capsule for two hours with nothing particularly interesting to talk about and still make us care? Let Oliver Stone

try it—and he's won *twice* for Best Director.

The reason I bless the Academy for snubbing Ron Howard should be clear: *We now have something new to bitch about.* Charlie Chaplin never won a competitive acting award? Garbo was ignored? Cary Grant got stiffed? Personally, I wouldn't have it any other way. The fellow getting the most mileage out of injustice these days is Martin Scorsese, who lamented in a recent interview in this magazine that he felt underappreciated Out There. Personally, I don't think the very talented Scorsese even runs a close second to Stanley Kubrick. No director on my watch has been as hosed—*Dr. Strangelove* loses to *My Fair Lady*, *2001* loses to *Oliver!*, *A Clockwork Orange* loses to *The French Connection*. Yesss.

For me, Kubrick is the greatest working American director. And I hope he *never* wins. I don't want to give up my rage, don't you see? I want the Academy to continue its perfect, goofy ways. I want to continue to be baffled and dazed, heart-warmed and -broken.

Forever.

Now to this year's edition. Since you have either (a) gotten sick of it or (b) forgotten it by now, I promise to take less time than any of the five nominated songs.

1. Quincy Jones. Drag him back if need be.

2. Whoopi. Somehow she managed to seem both funny and, on occasion, wise as she tugged the festivities along. And whoever wrote her opening ribbon rift should get kisses on both cheeks.

3. Vanessa Williams. How do you sing like that *and* look like that and *not* be a Hollywood star? I would put her in a lot of movies and make a lot of money.

4. Sharon Stone. Her "All right, let's all have a psychic

moment" was the ad-lib of the night. (The envelope had been misplaced.) How do you make a joke like that *and* look like that and not be a comedy star? I would make her stop killing people and put her in a lot of comedies and make a lot of money.

5. Christopher Reeve. Shocking and of course moving, and suddenly I was in London, maybe a dozen years ago, where he was doing a play on the West End. *The Princess Bride*, which I wrote, had come alive, and he was interested in talking about playing Westley, the hero, so we met and spent a little time together.

And I remember thinking what an unusual young man he was. For a star, first of all, he was a serious actor. And he was also seriously tall. (Most stars tend to be *waaaaaay* smaller than you imagine—which is why they all wear boots, and why they wear them all the time.) And Reeve was polite. And book-intelligent. And there was about him an undeniable decency. And watching him in his imprisoning chair Monday evening, I thought, *There are so many horrible human beings who lucked into being movie stars—why did God have to select one of the fine ones?*

6. Emma Thompson. The major acceptance speech of the night. She embraced Tony Hopkins, her presenter, and she started to speak, all trembly and moved. "Before I came," she said. "I went to visit Jane Austen's grave . . . in Winchester Cathedral . . . " At this point, *groans* had begun all across America. And at *this* point, her timing blissful, Miss Thompson knocked us all for six by adding: "to pay my respects, you know . . . and tell her about the grosses."

Maybe there's something to be said for a Cambridge education after all.

7. Kirk Douglas. I wonder what any young viewers still awake must have thought. Because Douglas was never thought of as being a great "actor" and was not really even a giant box-office star, like John Wayne.

But Christ, did he have power. And watching him all but *run* from the wings at 79, still tough and sassy, still ready to fight any man in the house—well, I've always been a huge admirer of Douglas, but never more than when I watched him take the stage last Monday.

8. Meryl Streep. The shock on her face when *Braveheart* won Best Picture summed up the night for me. Because of course it was a surprise, on an evening of surprises—and maybe the biggest surprise was just how swell the show was. Funny, sometimes, and sad—that too. It had everything—*except quality films from major Hollywood studios.*

There were quality films, all right. From Australia and England and Italy—and from the lesser American distribution companies. But almost none of the majors.

The big studios have gone into the junk business now.

It wasn't always like this. Out of curiosity, I looked to see who won in 1946. Understand something: This was not considered a great year back then. Not like '41, which had *Citizen Kane* and *The Maltese Falcon* (neither of which won Best Picture). Or 1940, which had *The Philadelphia Story* and *The Great Dictator* and *The Grapes of Wrath* (none of which won Best Picture). Or 1939, which had *The Wizard of Oz* and *Stagecoach* and *Wuthering Heights* and *Of Mice and Men* and *Goodbye, Mr. Chips* and *Ninotchka* and *Mr. Smith Goes to Washington* and *Gunga Din* (none of which even came close to winning Best Picture, because it was the year of *Gone With the Wind*).

No, 1946 was just this sunny happy year, the first Oscars after the war ended. Still, it brought us *Notorious* and *My Darling Clementine* and *The Big Sleep* and *Gilda* and *The Postman Always Rings Twice* and *The Killers* and *The Stranger* (none of which, by the by, even got *nominated*).

But *The Yearling* did. As did *The Razor's Edge*. And

Henry V. Not to mention *It's a Wonderful Life.* And the eventual winner, *The Best Years of Our Lives.*

We are on a slippery slope, folks, and if the major studios feel the least bit ashamed, well, why shouldn't they—whose fault is it? And if you think I'm being too negative, try this nightmare thought: What if this past year, this *annus horribilis*, turns out to be the *best* of the rest of this century?

Three final hopes and prayers.

1. Now that Michael Ovitz has left the agency business, the media are hustling to find a replacement (an ex-model with William Morris is an early contender). Please tattoo this inside your eyelids: *Agents do not matter.* They never have. They never will. Talent matters. Agents just live longer.

2. Can we please have a moratorium on awarding drunks, hookers, and the intellectually challenged? These are the easiest parts in the world to play and require the least acting skill.

3. Most fervently, can the Academy stop milquetoasting and *please let us know the actual vote tallies?* Not during the show but right afterward. Can you imagine our anger, our shock, our interest, our joy? We would—and I mean this—talk of nothing else but movies around the water cooler for days.

Which is, after all, what Hollywood wants us to do anyway.

—APRIL 8, 1996

THE SUMMER SO FAR

THE LESSON OF MISSION: IMPOSSIBLE *AND* TWISTER*? IT*
WILL BE A GREAT SUMMER FOR THE STUDIOS, BUT NOT FOR
MOVIEGOERS.

Twister and *Mission: Impossible* are already joined at the hip—as if they were one movie with a four word title. Magazines and newspapers continually link them, alerting us to the fact that they are two of the fastest-grossing hits ever. They are not, of course, even remotely similar, and what they have to tell us about what we want to see could not be more different.

Mission: Impossible is as good an example as any of why studio executives have cornered the market on sedatives. As the world well knows, these bright men and women, brutally over-worked, living in a constant state of terror of replacement, have but one goal in life: *to save their own asses.* And the easiest way to ensure they do that is with a string of commercial films. So why are they suffering?

Probably you did not know this, but it is true: Movie stars, by and large, do not want to appear in commercial films. Keanu Reeves has just hopped off the *Speed* bus. Val Kilmer chose to start a franchise with *The Saint* rather than continue one with *Batman.* Every time this kind of thing happens, executives die a little.

Because they know this: If a wonderful actor like Jeff Bridges had played the lead in *The Fugitive*, it would have been successful. But with Harrison Ford it was gold. *Mission: Impossible* would have worked with Dennis Quaid. But box-office records might not have been toppled.

This is the awful paradox of studio executives: They know that stars are essentially worthless yet absolutely essential. We can all list the star-driven movies no one went to see, and still their prices keep rising. Why? Because if you can get them to do something they don't much want to, something simplistic, something (ugh) commercial, everyone can smile. What *Mission: Impossible* reminds us of is the worldwide longing to see certain beautiful faces in certain kinds of roles, for a certain (brief) time . . . .

Twister.

Twister is the worst movie in the history of the world that I'm glad I saw. How about that moment when the dad gets jerked into the heavens to die, leaving behind a permanently traumatized little girl? And the Force 5 tornado sucking everything in its path? Great special effects. I also think that if you took every moment in the film without a wind machine—if you spliced all the book scenes together—even the toughest living spy would confess to anything rather than watch it twice. But that's okay, isn't it? It seems it will have to be.

Twister, of course, comes out of *Jaws*, and I want to talk about two memorable book scenes, one from each film. *Jaws* first. Maybe two thirds of the way through, Robert Shaw, Richard Dreyfuss, and Roy Scheider are chasing the giant shark. They have had initial combat with the enemy, it's dusk, and they are to spend the night and take up their battle again the next morning. They go downstairs. And for a very long time, guess what? *No monsters.*

They get drunk, laugh, compare scars. Then Scheider

asks Shaw about a scar on his arm. A pause. Shaw replies he got it aboard the Indianapolis. Dreyfuss just stares at Shaw now. Scheider asks what the Indianapolis was.

Then, for four minutes—an amazing amount of screen time in a thriller—Shaw talks. He tells us about that doomed ship, how it got hit on its return voyage after helping launch the Hiroshima bomb, how it sank in twelve minutes, how an hour went by before the first shark attacked, what it was like listening as they kept on attacking and the screams kept coming and the ocean was red and no one came to help until it was too late, until 800 men had been eaten alive. For me, one of the great scenes in movie history.

Okay, back to *Twister*. Again, three people in an enclosed space. Helen Hunt and Bill Paxton, who used to be married, in the front seat of a truck, chasing twisters. With them is Jami Gertz, Paxton's present fiancee, a therapist. She has been terrified once already by an earlier twister, and now she's way worse because Hunt and Paxton, who were calm the first time, are also terrified.

Gertz gets more and more frozen. *Cows* are being blown through the air in front of the truck. And the music is blasting and the cows are screaming and the storm is coming closer and at this moment, Gertz's cellular phone rings.

And she answers it! She pulls it out of her fancy purse and it's one of her patients having a bad day and Gertz says something to the effect that this isn't really a good time to talk—but she keeps on talking. *What kind of medical advice can she give when cows are flying through the air?* This scene is so mindblowingly awful I know I will never be able to forget it, just as I will never forget the *Indianapolis* sequence from *Jaws*. But for very different reasons.

For instance, let's flip the scenes. We're back in *Jaws*, the shark is attacking, it's smashing their boat, and they could die soon—and Dreyfuss's cellular phone rings? And he answers it? And it's one of his students having troubles back at his oceanography lab? And while the shark is crunching the boat, Dreyfuss tries to help the kid? We would have stormed the screen back in '75. We would have hooted and raged, and, trust me, Spielberg would have been back directing *Night Gallery* episodes and happy to have the job.

I don't much like movies these days. And I think these two scenes indicate why. Maybe twenty summers down the line, we'll have a sweet little film about killer tidal waves. And we won't have to bother with people at all.

Victor Hugo said armies could be resisted, but not an idea whose time has come. The pop-culture idea of our time hit Peter Benchley when he was thinking about a giant shark he had read about and these six words happened: What if the shark got territorial? From that came the novel, and from the novel the movie. Nothing has been the same since. Because *Jaws* opened for movies the vein of gold that is special-effects violence. What no one knew back then was how deep and insanely rich that vein was. As Twister proves, our cravings still go as deep.

One time, someone else will think six different words and pop culture will shift again and our era will then be looked back on as quaintly as we now view the Musical era, or the Western era, or the Silent era. Benchley had his breakthrough more than a quarter-century ago—an eternity in the world of pop culture. Right now, maybe something is circling over somebody's head. Frankly, I can't wait for it to land.

When I was a judge at Cannes, the head of the jury had us meet after every few films to pick what we thought would win. I would like to try the same thing for the coming Oscars. If nominations closed now, what films would you want nominated for Best Picture? I have only one nomination, *Fargo*. It actually made me proud to be in the picture business. And if Frances McDormand does not get a Best Actress nomination (My guess? She won't. The picture opened too early), something is very wrong somewhere.

—JUNE 24-JULY 1, 1996

You Go, Girls!

The enormous success of The First Wives Club *should have proved beyond a doubt that audiences love women's movies. So why do studio executives still not get it?*

I once asked my dear friend Ed Neisser, a money manager in Chicago, why the stock market had gone down that day. He said this: "Because it didn't go up."

And he was serious. His point being that the market behaves in ways unknown to man, but that those people who make their money in finance cannot admit to ignorance, so we hear the market went down on news of profit sharing or went up on news of profit sharing. Or fears the Fed would step in. Or fears the Fed would not step in.

All, he explained, total bullshit. Even the great Mr. Buffett has no idea what's happening tomorrow.

Which brings me to the happiest event of the fall, the success of *The First Wives Club*. Why happy for anyone but Paramount, which gambled on it? Two reasons.

1. Studio heads do not like women's movies. Because for the most part, they are not bloodbath action flicks, and stu-

dio heads love bloodbath action flicks because they think teenage boys in Asia will get off on the gore and save them their jobs.

Do you know the most unusual thing about the huge success of *Fried Green Tomatoes*? That there was no *Fried Green Tomatoes II*. And that is because studio guys will tell you this: It was a non-recurring phenomenon.

That is their excuse for everything that has a soft edge. *Driving Miss Daisy*? Even bigger hit, but a non-recurring phenomenon. Not only do honchos not want to make women's movies; they hate the idea of doing women's movies with stars like Hawn and Keaton and Midler. *No audience for them. These actresses were terrific once, but it's over.*

Guess what? When you can take in $19 million on a non-holiday fall weekend, it is definitely *not* over. And that amount of money cannot be overlooked. Which is why there will be other movies trying to tap the same vein.

I wrote this years ago: *Nobody knows anything*. True then, truer now. *Twister* was a huge hit with Bill Paxton in the lead. Well, believe this—the studio guys would have been happier if Harrison Ford had played the part, because then their world wouldn't be shaken. They have cast their lot with stars. If Ford had played the lead role in *Twister*, the wisdom would have been as follows: "Sure, he may be a little long in the tooth for romantic comedies like *Sabrina*, but put him in an action flick where he is one guy going against giant forces, like in *The Fugitive*—the guy is box-office gold."

Tattoo this behind your eyelids: *The picture is the star.* And has ever been.

2. The second reason for cheer is seasonal. We all know Hollywood makes too many movies. To ensure disaster, it also

groups most of what it hopes are its biggies at two times—early summer and Christmas.

And why? Well, because it does. (The market didn't go up today because it went down, remember?) My biggest movie laugh in weeks was when *Variety* reported that several unnamed Hollywood wise men said that *The First Wives Club* would have been even bigger if it had opened in the summertime.

Twits.

It would have been buried in the summertime, lost in the testosterone wilderness. Why did he say that? Because he believes it. He has to believe it. Because he cannot admit he has zero idea why the market behaves as it does.

I think the powers have to pay financial attention to $19 million. And somebody else may suck it up and try the same thing, and open his movie in October or April. Why, hit movies just might open all year long. Wouldn't it be nice if Hollywood became a twelve-month business?

When I watched *First Wives Club* and those three wonderful ladies flounced out the door and up the street belting out Lesley Gore, the audience burst into applause.

I was right there with them.

—OCTOBER 14, 1996

WHO KILLED HOLLYWOOD?

Nineteen-ninety-six was the worst year in Hollywood history. Not *movie* history, mind you. Not in a year when *Fargo* came out. Not in a year that brought us *The English Patient, Shine, Secrets & Lies, Hamlet, Sling Blade, Lone Star, Big Night, Romeo+Juliet, Breaking the Waves* and *Looking for Richard*. All wonderful movies, but none of them Hollywood movies. The most startling and depressing thing about the recent Oscar nominations is not that *Jerry Maguire* was the only studio film to get a Best Picture nod. The crusher is that *Jerry Maguire* was the only studio film that *deserved* to get a Best Picture nomination. Even worse, everyone I know in the business agrees on just how shameful '96 was. Talk to any of the *Premiere* 100 types-off the record—and what you get is a sad nod of the head.

Should it matter where quality films come from? Probably not, but I was brought up in the '30s and '40s, and Hollywood films are the reason I've spent the last half of my life writing movies. And they used to be so wonderful.

Here are some of the films nominated for Oscars in 1954, the year I moved to New York and really began going to a lot of movies: *The Caine Mutiny, The Country Girl, On the Waterfront, Seven Brides for Seven Brothers, A Star Is Born, Carmen Jones, Sabrina, The Barefoot Contessa, Executive Suite,*

20,000 Leagues Under the Sea, *It Should Happen to You* and *Rear Window*.

Two observations about this list: (1) Most of these movies would win Best Picture *this* year, and (2) At the time, 1954 was not considered an outstanding year for movies.

So what happened?

There are many factors, none of them decisive alone, but when added together, you've got the potential for disaster. In no particular order they are: (1) art and commerce, (2) talent, (3) studio executives and (4) the Oscars.

Art and Commerce

Hollywood began as entertainment for illiterates.

A lot of it, of course, still is. (How else can you explain a studio actually greenlighting *The Fan*?) But running stride for stride with all the lowest common denominator stuff have always been—until this year—the occasional attempts at quality.

A studio head once said that when he made out his annual slate of films, he knew perhaps a quarter of them would tank, but he felt that the vast majority would do well and save his job. He also mentioned a special three. "Those last three," he said, "I have hopes for." He hoped they would be films he could be proud of.

Well, the studios don't want to make those "special three films" anymore. And nothing illustrates that point better than *The English Patient*. Producer Saul Zaentz—*One Flew Over the Cuckoo's Nest*, *Amadeus*, Best Picture Oscars for both—developed it, then took it to Fox, who initially agreed to put up the money. Not that much, in today's madness—maybe $30 million.

Then Fox changed its mind.

And the reason? They said they didn't want Kristin Scott Thomas as the love interest. But they said they would absolutely love to do it with Demi Moore. That killed the deal, and the movie eventually went to Miramax.

The Demi Moore story makes for good reading, but I simply do not believe it.

I believe Fox *said* it, and I believe they *meant* it when they said it. But I also believe that if Demi Moore hadn't been the deal-breaker, some other problem would have submarined the project for Fox.

Why do I say that? Because, among other reasons, Scott Thomas doesn't play the lead role. Fox's position would have made total sense if they had been nervous about Ralph Fiennes because he carries the movie. I understand the craving studios have for Big Stars who can pull at the box-office, and I confess that I am a fan of Demi Moore. (I even liked her in *Striptease*—how's that for an admission?) But look at her last four movies: *Now and Then, The Scarlet Later, The Juror* and *Striptease*.

None of those exactly exploded at the box-office, so we are not dealing with a Julia Roberts-*Pretty Woman* scenario. It makes no sense that Fox would insist on a certain star playing a certain secondary (though important) part for reasons of box-office appeal when that star is on a cold streak.

You know why I think Fox passed?

Best reason in the world: Demi Moore or no Demi Moore, they didn't want to make *The English Patient*. Which is their inalienable right, and no one can criticize them for that decision. *Why* didn't they want to make it? Because they don't want to be associated with *that* kind of movie.

And what is *that* kind of movie? To explain that, I need to talk about the difference between Hollywood films and what are now called "independent" films (and which used to be called "art" films). Hollywood films, in general, either want to tell us a truth we already know or a falsehood we want to believe in. *In other words, they reinforce.*

Jerry Maguire, a marvelous Hollywood movie, is a perfect example. What does it try to tell us? Two things: (1) If you're a really good moral guy, God will smile on you, and (2) Love will find a way. Do I believe those "truths" as I look around at the people I know? The decent ones in pain, and the pricks who are dancing? Do I truly think the meek will inherit the earth and that wonderful pudding-faced Renee Zellweger will snare the most desirable man alive?

Puh-leeze. But I want to believe them. And most important for the people who made *Jerry Maguire*, I *did* believe them while I was sitting in that theater. I laughed and cheered and teared up while I was sitting there: Can't ask for more.

Independent films—as a rule—have a very different agenda. I could take any of the other Best Picture nominations as an example, but I want to talk about *Fargo*, which was, for me, the movie of the year. What does that movie tell us? Well, as Frances McDormand leads us through the mayhem, several things. (And yes, I know I'm being simplistic.) It tells us there is justice on this earth and that evildoers will eventually be punished. Fine. We all want to believe that.

But *Fargo* also tells us that the wrong people die sometimes, that terrible things can happen to us. *Will* happen to us.

Independent films want to disturb us. They tell us things *we don't want to know*. I'm obviously making gross generalizations here—some Hollywood films are disturbing and some independent films are reassuring. But in general terms—and for the sake of this argument—that's the important difference between the two.

One last thing: I'm not talking here about the difference between entertainment and art. Hollywood films can be, and often are, art. And many, if not most, independent films are boring. Which brings me back to *The English Patient*, the kind of film studios don't want to make anymore.

The director most in my mind when I saw *The English Patient* was David Lean. I'm not saying it was even close to any of Lean's masterpieces, but it was working in his debt. Well, for more than a decade, Lean was Steven Spielberg in terms of box-office heat.

Would Fox have green-lighted Lean's *Bridge on the River Kwai* in 1996? Probably not with an aging English character actor like Alec Guinness, and maybe they'd have tinkered with the ending so that they didn't blow up the bridge. And they most certainly wouldn't have let William Holden's character die.

And what about Lean's *Lawrence of Arabia*? The greatest epic in the history of sound? An epic with an *unknown* in the title role? Playing a *homosexual*? A tormented one at that . . . who gets sodomized?

Are you out of your mind? They wouldn't even have let you on the lot to pitch that one. And why not? Because the studios have decided they don't want to make films that might have a special kind of quality. They only want to make films that are guaranteed to make them a lot of money.

I don't mean to imply that Fox is against quality—its big hit this year (and decade and aeon) was *Independence Day*, a terrific flick. *Independence Day* is one of my favorite comic-book body-count movies, but *The English Patient* is working a different side of the street: It doesn't want to make you scream, it wants to make you *think*. And studios today have no interest in that kind of story—at least not without what they call an "element." If they could have Mel Gibson in the lead and keep the budget at $30 million, they wouldn't have let you out of the room until they had made that deal. Same if Spielberg was attached to direct.

But right now, the kind of movies that made Hollywood *matter*—well, forget about them. They're gone. Gone because the men—and occasional woman—in charge have no interest in seeing them.

If any of this is construed as being critical of Fox, that's not intended—any of the studios could have had *The English Patient*. They all passed.

Nobody wanted it. Because it was risky, because it was foreign, because it was talky, because it had zero mindless violence, because it was intelligent, because you couldn't say what it was in one sentence. Who wants to be contaminated with something like that?

Art and commerce have been battling for 100 years in Hollywood, but these days, commerce is just wiping the floor with the other guy.

Talent

Talent tends to cluster.

Sophocles was not the only guy hustling his plays around Athens some 2,400 years back, and Shakespeare wasn't even the leading playwright of his time. The downside of this phenomenon is that there are fallow periods, and Hollywood is now struggling through a talent drought. We are not even close to having the number of really good writers we once had, and God knows we don't have remotely the number of quality producers.

This "talent gap" can be most easily demonstrated by considering our current crop of directors. There are a lot of good directors today, but only one great one—Stanley Kubrick, who doesn't work that often. Compare this to the astonishing number of great directors who were making movies when I first came to New York. (And keep in mind that I am not counting a lot of directors who were not involved with Hollywood financing or sensibility—Ingmar Bergman, Luis Bunuel, Rene Clair, Federico Fellini, Akira Kurosawa, Carol Reed and Jean Renoir, to name a few. And I am also not counting some old guys who were still capable of thrilling us—Frank Capra, Charlie Chaplin, Cecil B. De Mille.)

Here are some of the top directors working in 1954, and my favorites of their movies:

George Cukor: *The Philadelphia Story, My Fair Lady*

Michael Curtiz: *The Adventures of Robin Hood, Casablanca*

Stanley Donen: *Seven Brides for Seven Brothers, Singin' in the Rain*

Henry King: *Twelve O'Clock High, The Gunfighter*

Leo McCarey: *The Awful Truth, Going My Way*

Vincente Minnelli: *An American in Paris, Gigi*

Don Siegel: *Invasion of the Body Snatchers, Dirty Harry*

Robert Siodmak: *The Killers, The Crimson Pirate*

Raoul Walsh: *High Sierra, White Heat*

William Wellman: *A Star Is Born, The Ox-Bow Incident*

Robert Wise: *Somebody Up There Likes Me, West Side Story*

Pretty impressive, right? Okay, here's the kicker—*none* of these guys make my first team. I'm talking John Ford, I'm talking Howard Hawks and Alfred Hitchcock, Elia Kazan and David Lean, plus Joseph Mankiewicz, George Stevens, Billy Wilder, William Wyler and Fred Zinnemann. Back in the '50s, all these brilliant guys were turning out one film after another, some of them glories . . . and don't you wish even a couple of them were around today?

Studio Executives

One of the new words that is destroying Hollywood movies is *slot*. As in "Sly has a slot open this fall" or "Arnold just filled his spring slot." It refers to a block of time a star or director has available to make a movie.

What's so awful is that, when you are talking about slots, you are not talking about something else: *hunger*. I don't hear executives talking about making a movie they are dying to make. I was talking to a Major Star recently about one of his peers, a far finer actor but less of a box-office draw. The question was asked why the fine actor was making so much shit. "Listen," the Major Star explained. "Being a movie star has just become a pretty good gig." In other words, one of America's finest actors would never do a crappy movie for $750,000, but he's more than happy to do it for $5 million.

And studio executives know that. And they pray that stars sell tickets. Most of the studio guys I've met are really smart, but they don't care all that much about movies as movies.

As slot fillers, yes, As merchandising tie-ins—oh my—yes. As theme-park rides, you betcha!

And that's the problem. They are mostly ex-agents or business school types. They care about slots and profit and product and Burger King cross-promotions. But movies *aren't* a real business. Or at least they shouldn't be. When you make movies, you are dealing with a bunch of nut cakes who want to provide glorious memories for all those people sitting alone in the dark. As they once sat out there.

Amen to that.

The Cohns and the Zanucks and the Goldwyns hated agents and spat on MBA types, and they built Hollywood. Make your jokes about Louis B. Mayer, about Sam Goldfish, about any of them—but remember this: They lived above the store. And they loved movies.

And today, not one of them could get a decent studio job.

The Oscars

The first Academy Awards were held in the Blossom Room of the Hollywood Roosevelt Hotel. The date was May 16, 1929. A grand total of 270 people were in attendance. Dinner was served—either filet of sole *saute au beurre* or half a broiled chicken on toast—and none of the nominees were too nervous to eat because the winners had been announced three months earlier.

Today, it is not only the most famous awards show in history, it has become, for many people, a career crippler. Not for everybody, and not all the time. But look at what it has done to some of my favorite contemporary directors: Jonathan

Demme won the Oscar for *The Silence of the Lambs* in 1991. Here are some of the films he'd made between 1980 and 1991: *Melvin and Howard*, *Swing Shift*, *Something Wild* and *Married to the Mob*. In the six years since: *Philadelphia*. One movie—and he'd been working on that *before* he won the Oscar.

Sydney Pollack—Oscar: *Out of Africa*, 1985. In the twelve years previous to that, he'd done *Jeremiah Johnson*, *The Way We Were*, *Three Days of the Condor*, *Absence of Malice* and *Tootsie*. In the dozen years since, he has directed just three movies: *Havana*, *The Firm* and *Sabrina*.

Steven Spielberg—Oscar: *Schindler's List*, 1993. Before that, *Raiders of the Lost Ark*, *E.T.—The Extra-Terrestrial* and *Jurassic Park*. Since then? Nothing. Nothing at all. By far the longest dead spell of his career. *The Lost World*, his *Jurassic Park* sequel, is due this summer.

Quentin Tarantino—Oscar: *Pulp Fiction*, Best Original Screenplay (with Roger Avary), 1994. A brilliant beginning to his career, with one prior directing credit: *Reservoir Dogs*. Since 1994? Less than nothing. A one-quarter credit on *Four Rooms*, one of the worst ego flicks of the decade. If you still need convincing, try these:

Robert Redford—Oscar: *Ordinary People*, 1980. He waited *eight* years before his next directing job.

Warren Beatty—Oscar: *Reds*, 1981. He waited *nine* years before his next directing job.

James L. Brooks—Oscar: *Terms of Endearment*, 1983. Four years before his next directing job.

Milos Forman—Oscar: *Amadeus*, 1984. Five years before his next directing job.

Kevin Costner—Oscar: *Dances With Wolves*, 1990. Nothing since. Nothing at all. Seven years and counting.

Why these terrible silences? That's impossible to answer precisely, but two thoughts come to mind:

(1) These very bright men forgot one of the basic Hollywood truths: *It's only a movie.* You can almost hear their minds working—"Omigod, how do I top *Pulp Fiction?*"

As if anybody cares.

(2) What we're talking about here is an inflated sense of self-importance. And we're also talking about *terror*. One way or another, each of these guys was an outcast—they were clerks or acting teachers or movie stars exercising their egos. And they suddenly went from having their noses pressed against the Windowpane of Acceptance to being President of the Club.

Hard to adjust to that if your success has been based on *I'll show them!* And not only did you show them; they loved you for it! That's scary. That can cripple you.

Would these talented men have had the identical careers if they had *not* won the Oscar? Of course not. They would still be out there making movies. What we are staring at is a terrible waste of time and talent.

Is Oscar *totally* to blame? Of course not. *Partially?* I say yes.

The Wisdom of Chairman Clint

There is a sequence in a pretty good action thriller, *The Rock*, that I hated a lot. Briefly, Nicolas Cage, an FBI man, has Sean Connery released from prison because he needs Connery's help. Connery insists on being pampered at a first-class hotel, with room service, a tailor, the works. Then Connery escapes. With Cage in hot pursuit.

The ensuing car chase seems to destroy most of the city of San Francisco. It goes on and on and on, and I remember thinking as I watched: Connery *has* to get away because, if he's recaptured, the whole thing was pointless and should have been cut. Guess what? Cage recaptures Connery.

I was describing my anger at this sloppiness to Clint Eastwood one day. "It's crazy," I said. "He already *had* Connery as a prisoner, so the entire car chase turned out to be simply a waste of movie time and millions of studio dollars. It made no sense."

Eastwood, who is smarter than most of us, looked at me for a moment, then said, "Bill, today the car chase *is* the sense."

Since the world has gone star-happy, maybe it's appropriate to end this discussion with a few words about Dennis Rodman. Rodman—who was suspended for kicking an innocent photographer in the nuts—is a great rebounding and defensive forward currently in the employ of the NBA's world-champion Chicago Bulls.

He is now a genuine media star, with commercials and magazine covers and bestselling books and movie and television deals and, from time to time, basketball. And he is making a terrible mistake: He thinks he is loved for his escapades, but everything coming to him now comes not because of his dresses or hair coloring, it comes *because* of basketball.

I don't mean to get apocalyptic, but I think Hollywood is making a similar mistake. The studios have forgotten that movies had better thrill us here—in America. The reason they make comic-book bloodbath pictures is simple and businesslike—there is an audience for them abroad. The biggest-grossing films of last year, *Independence Day*, *Twister*, *Mission: Impossible* and *The Rock*, all performed better overseas than they did here—at last count, by at least $335 million.

The studios are making movies today for mouth-breathers in foreign lands, testosterone-filled young men who get off on the violence. Why is that a problem?

A young friend of mine was going through the movie ads last weekend with his girlfriend. They turned the pages in silence until he looked at her and said, "I don't *want* to go to a Hollywood movie." I hated hearing that. The studios should tremble when they hear that.

The people behind every dominant entertainment form of the twentieth century have been arrogant enough to think that they will last forever. This was true for vaudeville, then Broadway, then radio and network television. Unfortunately, the people who make movies *still* think that way.

But what if they keep green-lighting the same garbage they have in recent years? The executives in charge may save their jobs—for the moment—but what if the American public turns away? What if my young friend is the start of a wave? What if '96 turns out to be Hollywood's high-water mark? What if, after the volcano flicks and the twister sequels, the audience starts looking elsewhere?

Audiences have done it before.

What the 1996 Best Picture Nominations Mean

Having thoroughly depressed myself, I can now move on to something sunny—this year's nominations. I was thrilled by them. And shocked by them. For weeks I had been telling anyone who would listen that all the media hype about this being the Year of the Independent was just that: media hype.

I was saying that because the Academy Awards are *Industry* awards. The *Hollywood* industry. And just as Detroit is not likely to declare some heap from Korea its car of the year, I thought it inconceivable that voters would honor, say, a low-budget Australian movie about a deranged piano player.

But they did. Somehow they did. In fact, they honored four movies—*The English Patient, Fargo, Secrets & Lies* and *Shine*—whose combined budgets weren't half of what Michael Ovitz got for leaving Disney. Does this mean anything?

Probably not. I have heard two explanations for these nominations. The first is that the Academy has been skewing younger—a lot younger—and all those hipper members finally made the difference. I guess that's possible.

The second explanation is those "For Your Consideration" cassettes mailed to Academy members. They have been around for years, but this year more than any other, people were talking about the offbeat. And folks who ordinarily would not have yawned in the direction of *Sling Blade* heard enough about it to at least slip it into their VCRs and watch. And be moved by what they saw. That was certainly a factor.

But I think there's another explanation. I think all of us who are members, all of us eligible to vote this year, all of us who live for and care about Hollywood movies—I think we all sat down and sucked it up and screamed at the Powers That Be: "STOP MAKING SHIT!"

That's what I think the nominations mean.

—APRIL 1997

THE FOLLOWING WERE ACADEMY AWARDS FOR 1996:

Best Actor	*Geoffrey Rush, Shine*
Best Actress	*Frances McDormand, Fargo*
Best Director	*Anthony Minghella, The English Patient*
Best Picture	*The English Patient*

AND WHERE WILL YOU LEAVE JIMMY STEWART?

And where will you leave Jimmy Stewart?

In despair, about to jump off the bridge in *It's a Wonderful Life*, just before Clarence comes? Or in triumph, at the very end, holding his family, saying "That's right, that's right" as his daughter tells him an angel just got wings. Or drunkenly holding Katharine Hepburn in *The Philadelphia Story*, his only Oscar-winning part. Or wheelchair ridden, snooping with binoculars, in *Rear Window*?

We will all leave him somewhere.

I believe this: that the great stars provide us a legacy, a blizzard of images to remember. But one of those images—and its a different one for every fan—is most important to us. And it is in that place that we park the stars, until we need to summon them back into memory.

In no particular order then:

For **Cagney** it's the end of *White Heat*, the greatest gangster film. "Made it Ma! Top of the world!"

Marilyn? I would like to say on the table in *Bus Stop*, her finest work, but I can't. Standing over the subway grating, her skirt blowing up, that's where I always first find her.

Alan Ladd's probably more important to me than he is to you, but he's waiting in the saloon in *Shane*, **Jack Palance** staring across, as Ladd says, "I hear you're a lowdown Yankee liar." And then o then the roaring of six-guns.

Audrey Hepburn is a toughie. So many choices. *Sabrina? Breakfast at Tiffany's?* Got yours? Mine's the picture that made her a star, *Roman Holiday*, the press conference at the end when she's asked her favorite city and she starts into her prepared text about how all the cities are equally wonderful — but then she spots Gregory Peck standing there and she looks at him, says three words: "Rome. Definitely Rome." I will leave her there, thank you very much, only this time she's looking at me.

Gable. I have an odd place for him. Not hitchhiking with Colbert in *It Happened One Night* or saying goodbye to Leigh at the end of that Civil War thing. No, mine is in the very flawed *Misfits*. (And this is going from decades-old memory.) But he played an aging cowboy and he's in some not very big town and he thinks that his son is ignoring him and this is where I leave Gable, pounding on a car roof, shouting for his child, because as I sat in that 1961 movie theatre I realized something sad and it was this: Gable could act. After an entire career of being mainly irresistible, he shocked me revealing a talent for pain I never dreamed existed inside him. And never revealed again because he was dead soon after the movie finished filming. Which only made this moment sadder still.

Cooper. He probably wouldn't like it but it's *Sergeant York* when he's imitating a turkey gobbler.

McQueen. Becoming a star by riding the motorcycle in *The Great Escape*.

Kelly is obvious. Singing in the rain in *Singin' in the Rain*.

Astaire is obvious too.   Ginger in his arms, both of them turned out so perfectly, Gershwin playing, or Kern, or some other giant, as these two giants fly across an infinite dance floor, never bothering to touch down.

Tracy. So much to choose from, but for me it has to be with Hepburn, when he swats her on the ass in *Pat and Mike*.

Wayne. Walking. Just walking.   In any Western you want.

I don't usually leave the living, they might do something more indelible, but I'll gamble on these:

Brando, forever in the back seat of the cab in *On the Waterfront*, telling his brother (Rod Steiger) he *coulda been a contender*.   (This memorable scene is distinguished even more by one of the nuttiest pieces of production design ever—it takes place in the only New York taxicab in history with venetian blinds over the back window.

Pfeiffer. 'Makin Whoopee' on the piano top in the *Fabulous Baker Boys*.   I met her once and asked her about that moment, about what was going through her mind when she did it and she said this: "I was thinking, Michelle, whatever you do, don't fall off." And yes, she is that beautiful.

Liz. Staring dead at the camera in *A Place in the Sun*, saying, shocked and perfectly gorgeous, "they're watching," (And Monty I leave, staring at Liz in that same scene in that same glorious movie.)

What about **Mitchum?** For me, the most underrated actor. I pick a moment not of violence nor of cynicism but gently romantic.   In a forgotten little movie, *Rachel and the Stranger*. When, in a sweet light voice, Mitchum sings.

Bill Holden. Running at the Kwai Bridge shouting "kill him."

And **Bette**? Has to be when she warns us to fasten our seat belts the night is going to be indeed a bumpy one. Of course, *All About Eve*.

Quickly now—**Welles** managing to mutter "Rosebud."

Leigh—Janet enjoying that nice warm shower . . . for awhile.

Chaplin—the end of *City Lights*, the terrified smile.

Fields—battling the blind man in *It's a Gift*.

Fonda—dancing with Cathy Downs, kickin' up his heels—literally—in *My Darling Clementine*. (And **Victor Mature**, helping the old Shakespearean actor finish his speech in that same classic western.)

Errol—fencing to the death down the giant staircase in *Robin Hood*.

And what about **Bogart**? My number two guy. Do I leave him in the *Maltese Falcon*? Easy enough to do. But what about when he went back into the leech infested water in *The African Queen*? But what about — no, too many of them. My pick? Storming out toward Dooley Wilson, then realizing, a moment later, why that particular song was being played. The look on Bogie's battered face. When he sees Miss Bergman. How could I not leave him there?

Now **Cary**. My all-time favorite. Was any actor ever blessed with more marvelous women? Do I leave him with Katherine Hepburn in *Bringing up Baby*, trying to help her cover the rip in her skirt, or being shot with a water pistol by Audrey Hepburn in *Charade*? Or sharing a chicken leg with Grace Kelly in *To Catch a Thief*? Or rescuing Ingrid in *Notorious*, or Eva Marie in *North by Northwest*?

I leave him with a guy, Sam Jaffe. Grant, wounded and helpless, lies by the temple of gold. Looking at the little water carrier, Gunga Din, and whispering these words: "The Colonel's got to know." Sending Din to his final fatal climb, at the climax of what is for me now and forever the movie of all time.

And where do I leave Jimmy Stewart?

In 1991 I turned 60, and went to Africa with friends. Our guide was the perfect Tor Allen, who had been Stewart's guide. And one night, Aug. 12, my birthday, we were sitting around a fire late. In Kenya's Masai Mara. Tired and happy, watching the fire weaken while nearby, we could hear the lions. We sat there quietly until Tor left us for a moment, then returned, holding a small tape machine. "I though you might like this," he said. And he pushed the play button.

And there in the middle of the night in the middle of Africa, suddenly came Jimmy Stewart's wonderful American voice. Scratchy, sure. Old, sure. But still strong. He was reading his poetry out loud. And as I listened I knew that this was where I would leave that splendid man. I had to. It was so perfect even the lions got quiet. At least I like to think they did.

No, I'm sure they did.

—JULY 13, 1997

A FILM FESTIVAL OF DIM BULBS

A decade past I was a judge at the Cannes Film Festival. My memory is we saw 22 movies in 11 days. I did not know then that the festival, in order to build suspense, tended to keep its better movies until the end. Ettore Scola, the Italian director who was our head, decided we should get together every three days—six movies—to discuss what we had seen.

The first meeting was agony. We groaned about how disappointed we were. After letting us vent awhile, he brought us up, *very* sharply, by saying this: "New rules. My rules. I declare the Festival over. We have seen all we shall see.

"*Pick your winners. Right now.*"

We only *thought* we had been in agony.

Okay. The Hollywood year is now two-thirds done. The key word here is *Hollywood*. I am talking studio films. I am saying this: "New rules. *My* rules. *I* declare the Oscar year over. We have seen all we shall see. Pick your five Best Picture Nominations. *Right now.*"

Think, fellow movie nuts.

Think about what we have been given thus far.

Think real hard.

Dot . . . dot . . . dot . . .

Do you get it?   Last year was the worst year in Hollywood history. This year, so far, is waaay more disgraceful.

Got your five yet?

Let me help—you won't. And why? *Because there aren't any*. Not any flicks we can see and shout, "Yesss! This is why I love the movies."

Donnie Brasco? A solid noninsulting gangster flick. Did you love it?   *Breakdown*?   A noninsulting little suspense thriller—for a while.   Then for a climax it went nuts with a James Bond truck fight. *Men in Black*? A super first half. But what kind of world are we entering when *Men in Black* is thought of as a prize winner? *Contact*? Jodie Foster will get nominated for Best Actress, and she should. David Morse, who played her father, won't get nominated for Best Supporting Actor, and he should. Their scene on the beach is the best dramatic scene of the year for me.

But it takes light-years for *Contact* to get there. It has all kinds of story problems culminating in an insanely stupid detour where I am asked to believe that Tom Skerritt is going into space when I have seen the billing and *I know* it will be Jodie alone facing the universe.

Them's the cream, folks.

You do any better?

Almost as disheartening is the *kind* of movie the honchos green-light.

When I was a kid I used to love Saturday afternoon serials. Buck Rogers, Tom Mix, Dick Tracy. Cheap and dopey and, to my 10-year-old eyes, Nirvana. You probably don't know them, but this is the kind of scene I mean—we're watching a Dick Tracy serial.

Lefty and Big Boss are cowering in a cellar somewhere trying to escape the relentless Tracy:

LEFTY: "Boss, boss—dis Tracy guy won't stop. How we gonna get him off yer trail?"

BIG BOSS: (The light bulb goes on!): "I got it, Lefty! We'll go visit dis sawbones I know. He'll save me."

LEFTY: "But how, boss?"

BIG BOSS: "We'll switch faces—see, he'll give me yours and you'll take mine, and I'll be safe robbin' banks cause Tracy'll be after you!"

LEFTY (In awe!): "Boss, dat is a genius notion." (And off they go to see the sawbones.)

Well, much as I hate to disagree with Lefty, that is not a genius notion. It is insanely silly. It is stupid. It would, however, have been perfect for us amazingly unsophisticated 10-year-olds half a century back.

And now?

Now they spend a hundred mill making it and guess what—they sure didn't underestimate the dumbness of the public—because *Face Off* is a hit.

And even worse, it was generally *endorsed* by the critics—because of the director John Woo. Woo is the Hong Kong bloodbath king. I like his stuff—if you're in the mood for crunchy over-the-top violence, Woo rates right up there. But puh-leese, critics, don't give me ballet comments and artsy parallels. Let him be what he is—a gore guy.

My favorite press release of the year came from the legendary Roger Corman, who announced a series of action flicks.

(This came after the success of *Air Force One*.) Corman, bless him, has a radically new and different hero: *a fighting Pope*. This particular cleric is not only the spiritual leader of millions, he is also a karate whiz. Biggest laugh I've had all summer.

But what's going on in Hollywood today is not, alas, funny at all. And I hate singing this song for two reasons—I've sung it before and it makes me seem as if I'm endorsing Deeply Important movies.

And I'm not. I think the greatest movie ever made is *Gunga Din*.

Which came out in that legendary *Gone with the Wind* year, 1939.

But I am *not* suggesting we go back to those days. They were great but they were then.

But how about going back even 10 years? Anybody who's reading this was watching flicks in 1987. Well, these are some of the movies released that year—and remember, it was not thought of then nor should it have been, as an outstanding year. But this is what the honchos used to greenlight only a decade past.

Baby Boom, The Big Easy, Broadcast News, Cry Freedom, Dirty Dancing, Empire of the Sun, Fatal Attraction, Full Metal Jacket, Good Morning, Vietnam, Hope and Glory, House of Games, Ironweed, La Bamba, The Last Emperor, Lethal Weapon, Moonstruck, Nadine, Predator, Planes, Trains and Automobiles, The Princess Bride, Radio Days, Raising Arizona, Robocop, Roxanne, Street Smart, Three Men and a Baby, Throw Momma from the Train, Tin Men, The Untouchables, Wall Street, The Witches of Eastwick, and *The Dead*—my personal pick for movie of the year.

That's 32 by my counting. No, not a great year. But it sure looks pretty mouth-watering today. Understand something—most of those pictures don't get green-lighted today.

Wouldn't appeal to the young men in Southeast Asia, who more and more—believe this—control what we see here in America.

Look, I understand that the studios are in business really for one great and good reason—to make money. I have no problem with any of that. But—big BUT—they are *not* making money with the stuff they are putting out today. You will, I am sure, have read how this was the largest-grossing summer in history. True.

But—huge BUT—*attendance is down.*

Those box-office numbers you read represent only one thing: *inflation.* And what I fear is that the studios continue to give over their product to the mindless, to the gigglers, to the people we skirt very carefully when we meet them on the street.

Hey, the Internet is here. And no one says we have to go to the movies.

In case anyone gets the idea I'm anti-Hollywood—the reverse, actually, but in any case, all is not lost—the worst movie of the year was neither American nor new; it was *Contempt*, the revival of a Jean-Luc Godard film from the '60s. I would rather have root canal than sit through it again. (And remember I wrote *Marathon Man*—I am not your calmest guy in the chair.) *Contempt* is endless pretentious garbage.

Of course, the critics thought it was the greatest thing since sliced bread. The most disgraceful piece of writing I've come across this year appeared in *The New York Times.* An incoherent multicolumned rave by one Philip Lopate. I have never met him, know nothing about him, but he's writing a book of film criticism.

You have been warned.

—SEPTEMBER 7, 1997

Rocking the Boat

December saved us this year, saved us from an even more awful moviegoing experience than that of 1996, which was the worst in Hollywood history. The Oscar nominations came out this morning, and what follows is essentially my view of the madness. And, sometimes, who I think is going to win and why. Before we open fire, a few things to bear in mind:

1) There is no "Best." Last year I thought *Fargo* was *the* flick. *The English Patient* took the crown. Doesn't make me wrong. Doesn't mean I'm right, either. Last year I thought the most putrescent effort was *Twister*. (I will never get over the scene in which a cow is flying past and the dumb lady shrink is on her cell phone talking to a patient. Disgraceful.) But I'll bet there are people who thought that *Twister* got robbed, that it should have been nominated. Are they wrong? Nope. For all we know, in 50 years there will be doctoral dissertations on such diverse subjects as "Symbolism of the Flying Cow in Fact and Fiction" or "The Behavior of Women in Windstorms."

2) A lot of people wonder: Do voters take the awards seriously? Know this: These awards *matter*. To those who win and to those who don't. When you leave these days, the first line of your obit will read, "Academy Award winner so-and-so died today."

When I was nominated for *Butch Cassidy and the Sundance Kid*, I watched the awards at home, in New York City, on the tube. Why didn't I go? Because I thought I'd lose, because I was obsessed with the Knicks' first championship run. But also this: The Oscars were not such a deal then. But they sure are now. When I was a kid, novels were important, theater was important, movies were our secret pleasure. Now, movies are the center of our culture. And the Oscars are the central awards.

Lives will change—I mean that—over who did or didn't get nominated, over who loses or wins. So you'd better believe this voter takes it seriously. Very.

3) I am looking for a flick that moves me while I'm there watching, but more importantly, a story that will surround me with memories as I age.

4) I have written about the Oscars before, and I always include this plea: For chrissakes, *let us know the votes*.

Here we go.

As Good as It Gets

Just a wonderful flick. Different and nutty and moving. I think Jack Nicholson will win Best Actor. He gave his finest lead performance since *Prizzi's Honor*, a decade back. And you know what? Easy part. Bill Murray would have been terrific, or Robin Williams or Gene Hackman, or if you want to go young, Jim Carrey would have been sensational. If Nicholson doesn't win, my guess would be it's because of his swell behavior at the Golden Globes. If you want to know what movie stars are really like, rewind that and run it over and over. I won't vote for Nicholson for a different reason—because I took a solemn oath years ago not to vote for drunks or retards. The Academy, in its wisdom, thinks those parts are hard to act.

Horseshit. Actors kill for those parts. They love to slur and stagger and drool. *Look, Ma, I'm acting.* I thought, for example, that there *was* an Oscar-winning performance in *Rain Man*—only it sure wasn't Dustin Hoffman. It was Tom Cruise who made that movie work. He was the rock. He was the reason you believed.

And for me, now and forever, *As Good as It Gets* is about Helen Hunt. Before I get to why, a few notes and comments.

A lot of people found the opening slow. I think they're right, and I don't think there's a damn thing director James L. Brooks—brilliant, brilliant work—could have done. He had an odd story to launch, weird characters to set up, and that just takes time.

A lot of people found the movie too long. I think it just *feels* long, because screenwriters Mark Andrus and Brooks came up with a weak idea in the middle. The three stars (the third is Greg Kinnear, who is super) go off on a road trip, and the reason they go is so Kinnear, who's failing as a painter, can ask his parents for money. Well, I didn't want to take that trip. I thought it was beneath the dignity of Kinnear's character. The scenes on the trip were just as terrific as the rest of the flick. But hovering over them was the dreaded scene in which a guy I was rooting for had to beg. The fact that the scene never happens doesn't matter—I was told it was going to. And my interest did not sustain. If Andrus and Brooks had come up with a better reason for the trip, and changed nothing else, no one would have found the movie long at all.

Something that there is no reason for anyone not in the business to know is: *Movie stars happen by mistake.* Some star turns down a role, someone lesser gets it, the movie is a hit, and, "Hello, everybody, this is Mrs. Norman Maine." I have two favorites in this category. One is George Raft, who kept turning down parts—*High Sierra, The Maltese Falcon,* maybe

Casablanca—ensuring Bogart's immortality. But Montgomery Clift is the topper. Clift, mostly forgotten today, was the other great young acting star of the '50s, along with Marlon Brando. Clift turned down the William Holden part in *Sunset Boulevard*, the James Dean part in *East of Eden*, the Paul Newman part in *Somebody Up There Likes Me*, and the Brando part in *On the Waterfront*. If he had taken them, he would have gone down as the greatest star in the history of sound. And those other four bimbos? They never happened.

Holly Hunter turned down the female lead in *As Good as It Gets*. Over, apparently, money. Inconceivable, as Vizzini used to say. And why? Because Holly Hunter would have been brilliant in the part. It's a great part, a great *woman's* part, a ca-reer-resurrecting part. That's point A. Point B is this: James L. Brooks *made* her. *Broadcast News*, 1987. The door was left open.

I will be shocked if Helen Hunt isn't around for the next decade. She was the rock of this funny-sad movie. She made you believe. Nicholson got to not step on sidewalk cracks and be endearing; Kinnear got to play the tormented gay. She came into battle with really nothing. Except her talent. But she made you believe a lot of things: That she really was a waitress. That she really had a kid. That she really cared for him. That she really didn't care for the fact that he was sick. That the world had dealt her a shit deal.

But she played it as it laid. Plain. Funny. Wounded. Knowing. And if she doesn't get the Oscar, that scream of out-rage you hear on your TV set will come from me. If one of those Brits wins—because the Academy, in its "infinite wis-dom," thinks they are better than we are because of their ac-cents—I will personally track those members down and make them repent.

If this sounds like a love letter, it is.

The Full Monty

The anti-*Titanic*. Hollywood really liked this picture. Because it was cheap, because it did phenomenal business (especially overseas), and, most importantly, because everyone Out There is terrified of losing their job. (And they should be. They're all going to get fired. Sneered at. Banned from the new Spago.) *The Full Monty* snuck up on everybody, arms wide, laden with sweet surprises: the kiss, the moment in the police station when the men see themselves on tape and one criticizes another for his timing—this, when their lives are about to be ruined. And as far as I'm concerned, this is the one film that completely throws the Oscars up for grabs.

Now is as good a time as any to make clear why I think they have to let us know the voting tallies. One of the things that drives me nuts is when I read stuff like this: The Academy will most likely honor *L.A. Confidential* for Best Adapted Screenplay because it wants to reward the film and this is the best category." Total, total horseshit. Do you think all us old-fart voters get together and discuss fairness? Some ancient biddy gets up, using her cane, and says in her withered, cracked voice, "Should we give *L.A. Confidential* anything? It didn't do much business, but I think we ought to honor it anyway." Wheezes of agreement. Pacemakers whirr into overdrive. *You think that happens?*

But something has to win Best Picture. *Titanic* is clearly the favorite. Let's be Kremlinologists. A lot of people Out There are envious of *Titanic's* success. Before the nominations were made public, I thought *As Good as It Gets* was the one that might give *Titanic* the most trouble: And it could still win—but I don't think so. Because, in a disgraceful oversight, Jim Brooks did not get a director's nomination. I mean, three acting nominations, Best Picture, Original Screenplay—I guess it's just this year's Picture That Directed Itself. But what the oversight indicates is this: The depth of favor from the Academy is not enough for it to go all the way.

There isn't enough depth of favor for *L.A. Confidential* either: Not one male member of that triumphant cast was nominated. *Titanic* was hurt, too: Two other painful oversights were Leonardo DiCaprio's not getting a Best Actor nomination—like not recognizing Gable in *Gone With the Wind*—and James Cameron's being shut out on screenplay. Those omissions maybe tell us that the anger and envy against *Titanic* are surfacing.

That leaves *Good Will Hunting* and *The Full Monty*. *Good Will Hunting* has the Miramax publicity machine—the best there is—hyping it. People like it. It could win. *The Full Monty* has nothing going for it. No names anywhere, no special effects, zero. Perfect to fight *Titanic*. If anyone Out There wants to give it the finger, *The Full Monty* is that vehicle.

Do you see now how fascinating it would be if, the morning after the Oscars, we knew the votes? We could get angry or frustrated all over again—and talk about movies even more. Which is what Hollywood wants in the first place. All the stuff I just wrote here, total conjecture. We will never know how one movie affects another. And that's a damn shame.

I know nothing, but I think this: With *The Full Monty* on board, *Titanic* at last is vulnerable. (Almost said *sinkable*—now you know everything.)

Good Will Hunting

It was never meant to be a prizewinner. It was meant to jump-start the careers of the two terrific young actors who wrote it, Ben Affleck and Matt Damon. And I think they will win the Best Original Screenplay Oscar. (More about that, as they say, presently.) Full disclosure: I spent a day working with them on it, and thank God I didn't damage their talent.

You know how some people will recommend a book by telling you, "It's a terrific read"? Well, this is a terrific watch. Damon is going to be remembered for his performance for years, and Affleck's moment toward the end, alone on Damon's porch, was the most moving in the picture. And as I sat there munching my popcorn, do you know what movie was in my head? *Snow White and the Seven Dwarfs.* Why? Well, both Matt and Snow were orphans. Both had crappy manual jobs. Both were the least bit unusual in that she was the most beautiful woman in the universe, he the most brilliant man.

And they both had dreams. The handsome Prince answered Snow's, while Matt had to be satisfied with Minnie Driver, a Harvard senior on her way to Stanford Med. Better than ZaSu Pitts when you consider that Minnie is a) gorgeous, b) brilliant, c) with riches beyond counting. She also d) falls madly in love with Matt the minute she sees him out-smartass a smartass acquaintance of hers. Not to mention e) that her perfect love only swells as the story unwinds.

Now, I have met some Harvard girls . . . and they *weren't* like that. But Minnie is an everyday creature compared to Robin Williams, who gets to play one of Hollywood's all-time yummiest creations—*the shrink with only one patient!* Robin was put on Earth for this reason alone: to cure Matt Damon. And how does he do that? How does he take a tormented genius and wash his pain away? It is so easy, sports fans, that I think we should do this to all the disturbed and sad people we meet each day. Just tell them this: "It's not your fault." That's Robin's trick, anyway.

Saying it once, of course, won't do it. Matt is seriously fucked up. To cure any kind of mental torment, do it Robin's way. Tell this to Mozart, the next time you see him, or to that homeless guy babbling on the corner:

"It's not your fault.

"It's not your fault.

"It's not your fault.

"It's not your fault.

"It's not your fault.

"It's not your fault.

"It's not your fault.

"It's not your fault.

"It's not your fault.

"It's not your fault."

Pretty soon Matt is sobbing his pain away, and he and his shrink are hugging and making jokes, and God's sure up there in his heaven.

Listen, I *liked* this scene. And I liked this movie. But I won't vote it Best Picture.

Now to the Best Original Screenplay Oscar. Affleck and Damon wrote a wonderful script, but they will win because they are Affleck and Damon, because all of us want to glow in their warmth come awards night. It's just such a great *story*, dammit. Same reason Emma Thompson won. She wrote a wonderful script, but I think the reason she beat out *Apollo 13* and *Babe* was because she is Emma Thompson the star.

In other words, the dancing-bear syndrome. This is most grievously apparent with the Best Director award. When a star directs a quality film, the Academy goes nuts. "Ohhh, aren't they wonderful!" the Academy says. "How beautiful they are—aren't we lucky?"

There are some stars who are terrific *working* directors, such as Clint Eastwood. But most of them are Deities who only occasionally choose to come down and sweat. Warren Beatty has directed four films in twenty years. He won his first time out as a sole director, with *Reds*, in 1981. Know what I think? It was the *worst* directed of the five nominated flicks that year, the others being *Atlantic City*, *Chariots of Fire*, *On Golden Pond*, and, most brilliantly, *Raiders of the Lost Ark*.

Robert Redford has proved to be a world-class director. But he has only worked five times in eighteen years. And his first time out, he made a swell flick, absolutely as good as *Good Will Hunting*: *Ordinary People*. Do you know who he beat for Best Director? Martin Scorsese, for his masterpiece *Raging Bull*. I have never met Scorsese, but I'll bet that pain still burns him to this day. This is obviously not to blame Redford. It's the Academy.

And I think they will reward Affleck and Damon because they are becoming two wonderful stars. My problem is, and I will bet the farm as I am in my pit writing this, that they are not in their pit cranking out their next flick. Hope I'm wrong. I want to see it. I hear Emma Thompson is close to trying again. To which I say two things: 1) good, and 2) about time.

L.A. Confidential

The critics movie of the year. And a great torment when it turned out not to be a big hit. I, too, wish it had done better. It has just marvelous stuff. The look of it, the feel, the acting, script, and direction. But—it's confusing . . . it has a terrible ending . . . and it's phony.

The confusing charge I can sum up in one word: *heroin.* Did anyone understand that crucial part of the story? I sure didn't. I tried; I just couldn't make it make any sense. In truth, I didn't care all that much that I couldn't get it. I was well compensated. But I can't say the same for the other two points.

An ending is, for me, the most important part of a movie and the hardest to make work. I think the ending of *Butch Cassidy* is the best of any I've been involved with, but in truth, history took care of that for me. The worst ending of any great film is *Psycho's—seven minutes* of awful, awful psychobabble. (Rent it if you don't believe me.)

Well, in *L.A. Confidential* there is a super climax. A shoot-out in a motel. James Cromwell, the bad cop, shoots and kills Russell Crowe, the burly good cop. Cromwell and Guy Pearce, the uptight, brilliant cop, walk out of the motel into the night. Police sirens in the distance. Now lights. A memorable shot. Cromwell turns to Pearce, says, "Hold up your badge, so they'll know you're a policeman." And Pearce plugs the bastard in the back. Cromwell falls. Pearce takes out his badge holds it high. Final fade-out.

Oops, sorry—*should* have been the final fade-out. I think if it had been, I might have voted it Best Picture. *Six minutes* of anguish follow. Fatally damaging the film. But before I get into why that is, I have to talk about what I mean when I say the film is phony.

You can divide movies up any way you want, but one way is this: There are two kinds of films, let's call them Hollywood films and Art (or Independent) films. This is not about quality—I much prefer Hollywood films, and the best ones are, of course, art. And I find most Art films dull and pretentious. But clearly there are differences, and my definitions follow. Hollywood films want to tell us truths we already know or falsehoods we want to believe in. In other words, *they reinforce*. Art films want to disturb us, to tell us truths we don't want to know. In other words, *they unsettle*.

Okay, back to the flick. About 90 minutes in, this straightlaced, brilliant, tight-assed cop, Guy Pearce, fucks a third-rate whore. Something his character simply would never do. Why does he do it? Because she's not a third-rate whore, boys and girls, some scabby slut who's a Veronica Lake look-alike, she's—roll of drums, please—*Kim Basinger*. Well, of course he fucks her. My god, *she's a movie star*. Who could resist?

Well, he *must*. Because the character he's been playing would. (Snapshots are taken of their carousing, which spurs the plot. But they could have been taken of her just kissing him—before he rejected her.) Anyway, as I sat there, a deep chord of phoniness was struck. But I did my best to silence it till that awful ending, in which Pearce, the tight-assed cop, explains the entire plot—about which, believe me, we don't give a shit—and then the bad cops and the good cops get together and save all their asses. (Are your eyes glazing over reading this? Think what it was like sitting there.)

Anyway, after a few minutes of this madness, Kim baby appears. (By the way, she is just splendid in the part, her best work since *Nadine*.) And I thought, What in hell is she doing here? Then she leads Pearce outside—and my heart sank. Because Russell Crowe, the cop who was killed in the house, he *lived*. Cromwell, the most lethal and evil guy in all of L.A., *missed.* I'm groaning now. Crowe goes off into the sunset to live with Basinger, who—guess what—is a whore no longer.

I'm sorry, guys, you can't do that.

You can't work both sides of the street. The Art-film side—unsettles us, tell us that evil exists on Earth and we can't stop it and it's going to triumph. And the Hollywood side—whores have hearts of gold, skilled killers miss at point-blank when it's most crucial for them to shoot straight. And why? *So that true love will conquer.* Look, I wrote *The Princess Bride*—I believe in true love. And I *want* it to conquer. But *not* in *L.A. Confidential.* It is dead wrong here, it is phony here, and it kills what was and is a wonderful achievement.

Just not wonderful enough.

TITANIC

Maybe the most amazing thing about this amazing movie is this: the Billy Zane part. (For those eleven of you who have not yet seen the picture, Zane plays Kate Winslet's rich, cowardly, and in-all-ways-contemptible fiance.) I cannot think of another movie of this quality that has anything this awful near the core. Everything about the role—the writing of it, the directing of it, the *conception* of it—would have been unacceptable in an 1890s melodrama.

And why is that amazing? Because it doesn't matter. The central criticism that has been leveled at this movie is that the dialogue is cringe-inducing. Well, some of it sure is. Just one example, again dealing with poor mean Billy: Kate, unpacking in their suite, puts some paintings around the rooms to cheer herself up. Now, the way it's shot, we get to see snippets of the work. Not terrible stuff. Zane says, "God, not those awful finger paintings again. They certainly were a waste of money." Kate tells Billy that he has no taste in art, then says to the maid: "They're fascinating. Like being inside a dream or something. There's truth but no logic." The maid: "What's the artist's name?" Kate: "Something Picasso." Billy: "Something Picasso—he won't amount to a thing. He won't. Trust me." Kate, ignoring him, to the maid: "Put the Degas in the bedroom." Can you come up with another single scene with that many howlers? I can't. Not since the days of Joan Crawford.

But it doesn't matter. A word here about movie dialogue: *It is among the least important parts of a screenplay.* Sure, intelligent talk is always better than dumb stuff. And sure, dialogue matters more in some kinds of movies—wit comedies, such as *As Good as It Gets*, or intelligent dramas—than in others. But for the most part, the public and critics have come to believe that screenplays *are* dialogue.

Wrong. *If movies are story, and they are, then screenplays are structure.* And what makes this movie the unique experience that it is, is not Cameron's ear for dialogue or his skill at camera placement or his brilliance with special effects. It's his *storytelling*, folks. If *he* doesn't deserve a nomination for screenplay, no one does.

Titanic begins with some shots in black and white of the ship setting sail, people waving. Standard stuff we've all seen before. Snooze. Then the title appears and we are looking at the top of the ocean and we're in color. Hmm. I thought he'd stay in black and white longer. Now we're under the water and something is coming our way: a monster machine, a *modern* one. And we watch it approach a wreck . . . and then a shot of Bill Paxton squinting through a porthole . . . and I thought, Wait a minute, Bill Paxton is in this movie?

It was just the start of my education. Because what Cameron had done—and, for me, what makes this mother the great experience it assuredly is—is to have the old lady (wonderful Gloria Stuart) tell us about it. And then about eighteen minutes in comes this sequence that I will never forget. One of Paxton's underwater nerds shows Stuart, on a monitor, a digital re-creation of the ship sinking. It's all very cold and accurate and unemotional. And when it's over, Stuart looks at him and says, "Of course, the experience of it was somewhat different." And Paxton asks, "Will you share it with us?"

I think I started tearing up right about there. And throughout the ensuing swift three hours, I kept coming back to that re-creation. And dreading what was to come. Because a few minutes into the film, I knew everything.

And I knew nothing.

You will have read and will be reading why this movie is the freak that it is. But the only reason it's such a hit is this: *People want to see it.* Why was *The Postman* the biggest loser in history? *People didn't want to see it.* Everything else is mythology.

A young writer once said of Brando that the actor was just this tub who, he was told, once had talent. Then he went on to explain, *"I wasn't there."* By which I think he meant that when he saw Brando's young and legendary film work— *Waterfront, A Streetcar Named Desire*—he was looking at it through the gauze of time. And he's right—when we see *Gone With the Wind* today, we do not get the experience audiences did back in '39. Gable was alive then, vibrant then. When we see *King Kong* today, it kind of holds. But the special effects are creaky.

Well, in not many years, *Titanic* will look just as creaky to the audiences of the future. And the Billy Zane part will draw laughter, and people will look at each other and say, "This *worked* once? Audiences *believed* this?"

Yessir, we do. We believe the hell out of it.

Because every so often a movie comes along that has the courage to stand there and command this: "Look! Look at me! *See what I can do.*" Lucky for us that we were here, at this time, to watch . . . .

APRIL 1998

THE FOLLOWING WERE ACADEMY AWARD WINNERS FOR 1997:

Best Actor	*Jack Nicholson, As Good as It Gets*
Best Actress	*Helen Hunt, As Good as It Gets*
Best Director	*James Cameron, Titanic*
Best Picture	*Titanic*

THE EMPEROR'S NEW FATIGUES
(AND OTHER STORIES)

As everybody knows, studio executives spend fifty-one weeks a year making lowest common denominator flicks. The fifty-second they all take baths and try and smell nice.

Welcome to the Oscars.

What follows is mostly my feelings about the madness. Remember that *nothing* I say is remotely right. There is no right. Never forget this: the leading 18th century literary critics felt that the three greatest writers of all time were Homer, Sophocles and Richardson.

When I go to the movies, now and forever, I go as a virgin. I know as little as possible about what I am about to see. I do not read reviews, do my best to avoid the merciless hype that is now so much a dreadful part of our lives.

And what I want, now and forever, is this: *to be thrilled.*

One final thing you should know: for me, *movies are story.*

Oscar voters, for reasons known only to science, tend to vote for what I call *medicinal movies*. Movies, in other words, that are *good for you*. My theory is that if a medicinal movie is up against one that ain't, it will always win, not necessarily at the box-office, but in the voting. And if two equally medicinal movies vie, the biggest grosser gets the glittering prize.

None of my choices did well in the nominating process, since none of the three were medicinal. I thought the best foreign language film was *Central Station*, not *Life is Beautiful*. The best English speaking foreign film was *Waking Ned Devine*, not *Shakespeare in Love*.

And my choice for best picture was *There's Something About Mary*. I would have given it Best Actress and Best Screenplay as well. The Academy has always ignored two of the hardest genres to create: comedies and adventure flicks. *Shakespeare in Love* is certainly a comedy but the Academy may ignore that for this reason: it isn't funny.

Anyway, this year I am going to talk about the five Best Picture nominees in terms of highest medicinal value. Which is why they were nominated in the first place.

SAVING PRIVATE RYAN

The bullshit started early with this baby. I remember these remarkable interviews being given on the talk shows during the standard pre-opening hype. Sort of like this:

RYAN HYPIST   I have to tell you the most important thing of all.

GENERIC KATIE   Please.

RYAN HYPIST   (Pause) Well this movie, it's . . . um . . . violent.

GENERIC KATIE   (Nodding—fascinated) You mean . . . bloody?

RYAN HYPIST   Oh yes, oh God yes, bloody, so much blood, people getting blown up, killed—I have to tell you all this Generic Katie because I would *never* want to mislead the audience: this movie is a blood bath. Just so your audience knows that before they go—this movie is filled with battle scenes and gore and explosions and young men dying.

GENERIC KATIE   (moved) Thank you for being so . . . brave and honest with us. I know it must have been hard for you.

And I am staring at the tube thinking, *what is everybody smoking?* Let me put it another way. Let's say I am hyping a remake of *How To Marry A Millionaire*. But instead of a frothy comedy with Bacall and Grable and Monroe, I have made a hard R version. Starring Cameron Diaz and Heather Graham and Catherine Zeta-Jones.

MILLIONAIRE HYPIST   I have to tell you the most important thing of all.

GENERIC KATIE   Please.

MILLIONAIRE HYPIST   (Pause) Well, this movie, it's . . . um . . . sexual.

GENERIC KATIE   (nodding, fascinated) You mean . . . with nudity?

MILLIONAIRE HYPIST   Oh yes, oh God yes, passion, so much nakedness, people having orgasms—I have to tell you all this Generic Katie because I would *never* want to mislead the audience: this movie is carnal. Just so your audience knows before they go—this movie is filled with rapes and lesbianism and nipples and young women screaming with sexual pleasure.

GENERIC KATIE   (moved) Thank you so for being so . . . brave and honest with us. I know it must have been hard for you.

Sex and violence are the twin items Hollywood wants most desperately to sell these awful days. That's why the *Ryan* hype was so fraudulent. Here is the kind of brave and honest hype you will *never* live to see.

HYPIST   I have to tell you the most important thing of all.

GENERIC KATIE   Please.

HYPIST   (Pause) Well this movie, it's . . . um . . . philosophical.

GENERIC KATIE   (Nodding, fascinated) You mean . . . with talk?

HYPIST   Oh, yes, oh God, yes, tons of conversation, all of it dealing with pain and suffering and how to live on earth without doing harm. I would *never* want to mislead your audience: This movie is intelligent. Just so your audience knows before they go—this movie is thought-provoking and deep and filled with the kind of wisdom we so need on earth these days.

GENERIC KATIE   (To herself) Didn't believe one word.

Saving Private Ryan begins, as I'm sure everyone has told you, with an incredible battle sequence. Maybe that was true for them, but the version I saw sure began differently: a fifteen-second shot of Old Glory a-wavin' in the wind. With Copland-like music in the background. Even John Wayne would have been embarrassed to start a movie that way. Hearts and flowers, God bless America, all that awful stuff. Today, only the Farrellys could get away with something like that.

Then there follows a weird sequence which I have subtitled "The Man With the Big-Boobed Girls." And I am not being facetious. This old guy lumbers around someplace, we don't know where, and behind him are a bunch of Norman Rockwell types, but all I can concentrate on are these big-boobed girls who are tagging along. Then we find that we're in a cemetery, and a shot of a flag tells us France. Lots of crosses. He kneels, at a particular cross, weeps, some of the family run to him, the big-boobed ones hanging back.

Then a long shot of his moist eyes and as the camera moves slowly into a close up of those eyes, we know this much: *we are going into flashback now.*

The story that has moved this old man is about to be told.

And *now* we are into the battle sequence.

What to say about it? Fabulous, brilliant, extraordinary, whatever you want. And do you know why? The length: *twenty four minutes*. The stuff itself is absolute as good and no better than Francis Coppola's war stuff or Oliver Stone's war stuff. But here it just goes pulverizingly on and on. It was brave of writer Robert Rodat to write it that way and brave of director Steven Spielberg to direct it with that incredible relentless tension.

What to say about Spielberg? For me, as great a shooter as anyone in movie history. Clearly the most important American director of the last thirty years, and on occasion, the most brilliant.

When he is in his wheel house.

More of that presently.

As anybody reading this must know, Robert Rodat's story is about a squad of soldiers sent on a rescue mission—to find a Private Ryan, a young soldier who has lost three brothers in action. Ryan, once located, is to be sent back home before another tragedy totally destroys the remains of his family.

The last shot of the great battle sequence is a shot of a dead soldier named Ryan.

OK, so what the movie has to do is simple: *get the rescue squad going after the kid*. The Spielberg of *Raider's of the Lost Ark* would have taken maybe a minute to set that up. Tom Hanks, the squad leader would have been called into a commander's presence, told to find a Private Ryan. Hanks would ask why and the Commander would say what you know: to make sure he does not die like his brothers. Get him home *now* and get him home *safely*. Those are your orders. Go!

That is not a hard premise to set up. In this movie it takes Spielberg thirteen pretentious, operatic minutes. (An amazing length of movie time.) Climaxed when a General reads a letter Honest Abe Lincoln wrote which is soooo moving, sports fans, it brings tears to the other high officers who are listening to the General.

Sure.

Then, after more uninteresting stuff, *forty* minutes into the movie, Hanks' squad finally *finally* sets off on their odyssey to find Private Ryan.

And the hunt for him is just terrific. (A word here—he will not win the Oscar but Tom Sanders sure should—great production design.)

Sequence after sequence. The village with the French girl and the sudden Nazi's and the wrong Ryan. The church. The wounded area with the haunted pilot where they find out where Ryan might be. The bunker fight with the Nazi who Hanks releases and wonderful work between Tom Sizemore and Ed Burns and Hanks. Then the fight with the tank and offhandedly, surprisingly, they find Private Ryan.

We are an hour and forty five minutes into the movie now. We have just had an hour plus of sensational storytelling. And I am so excited because I *know* what is going to happen now: they are going to take Ryan back only it is going to be *so much harder* than finding him was. Maybe they would revisit some of the places—would the pilot have killed himself, would the French girl be killed by sniper madness, would the madness of the entire enterprise come crashing down around them? The story was going to be like a great snowball, accumulating as it roared toward climax, gathering weight and size and emotional power as Hanks desperately tried to get the kid home to his shattered mother.

And guess what: the rest of the movie is a disgrace. Fifty plus minutes of phony manipulative shit.

Things start going south immediately. We are in a

bombed French village which has a valuable bridge. Hanks tells Ryan to get ready. And Ryan—Matt Damon—says this: he doesn't want to go. Sure his mom has suffered, sure it's awful what's happened to his family, but these guys are his brothers now and he will not leave them.

Do you believe that? Do you believe that a young man who has just been informed his family has been devastated, that his mother has had grief overpowering poured on her, would say, hey, I'm sure mom'll understand but I want to stay here in the mud with my buddies.

Barely.

I can kind of make a case that Ryan is young and in such shock and feels so guilty at his good/bad fortune, he really at that moment wants to stay. OK. I go with that.

Then the first nail in the coffin: **Hanks goes along with it—hey, what a neat idea, I'll stay too.**

Inconceivable, as Vizzini would say.

Before I get to how it's done in the movie, let me make a parallel. Let's say you and I were given *a sworn task* by our father. To make sure little Matt next store gets to school that day. Our most important task on earth is to make sure that happens.

OK. We go to little Matt's house, tell him to come along. And he says this: "My best friend in the world is visiting me today. I won't go."

And you and I think about it and decide we have only *two* choices.

(1) To let him stay home.

(2) To stay home with him.

Take a second. That make sense? Are those the *only* two choices available? How about adding a third: *bringing the little fucker to school.*

In an awful awful scene, after Matt has stamped his foot in anger, Hanks and Tom Sizemore, the tough Sergeant have a talk.

Sizemore asks what Hanks' orders are and Hanks replies thusly: "Sergeant, we have crossed some strange boundary here. The world has taken a turn for the surreal."

And I am sitting there thinking no, nothing surreal about it. A simple request has been made that needs a simple answer.

Sizemore tells Hanks this. "Some part me of thinks the kid's right. What's he done to deserve this? If he wants to stay here fine. Let's leave him and go home."

And Hanks says "yeah."

And I say, where did the notion of *leaving* him and going home come from? Surely it has never been breathed on planet Earth before. *What are you talking about?* Then Sizemore hits him with the clincher: "But another part of me thinks what if by some miracle we stay and actually make it out of here? Some day we might look back on this and decide that saving Private Ryan was the one decent thing we were able to pull out of this whole God awful shitty mess . . . . We do that, Captain, we all earn the right to go home."

So they stay. (Sizemore's speech might have made sense earlier—when they were having the fight about staying or going home, earlier in the flick, before they had found Ryan.)

You know the worst thing? It would have been easy to have them stay and not be phony about it. How? Try this:

Matt makes his pitch. Hanks says I understand your emotions, but we're out of here *right now*.

Next cut, they are leaving the village.

Next cut they are crossing the bridge.

Next cut, walking in the countryside—

—and then a close up of Hanks and he stares and guess what?—

—*The Germans are coming*, They're *here*, it's *too late* to leave.

Next cut, exactly what we have now, and go on as before, only with more urgency. And without the awful manipulation.

The Ugly Tree

The most damaging speech of the movie comes next. Hanks and Matt Damon are waiting for the attack. Damon says he cannot summon up his dead brothers faces and Hanks says, think of something specific. Hanks, when he thinks of home, thinks of his hammock or his wife pruning the roses wearing his gloves.

And Matt Damon starts into this long—two minutes, folks—remembrance of the last time he and his brothers were together. A sexual escapade when one of his brothers was trying to fuck this girl, a girl who "took a nose dive out of the ugly tree and hit every branch on the way down."

The speech—ad libbed by Matt Damon is the only time we get to spend any private time with Ryan. And the speech does not exactly endear him to us. It also rips a lot of the emotional fabric of the film to pieces. I would love to know what the real script said at this point. And I wonder only this: how could Spielberg allow something this atrocious to happen?

The Shooting of Tom Hanks

A bunch of Germans come running toward camera. They get into prone position, start to fire. We are drawn toward one particular German bad guy. Want to know why? *He's the only one without a helmet.* And, gasp, we realize he is that very same Nodzi who Hanks let live in the earlier sequence. (Spielberg has just discovered irony.) And, shock of shocks, he is the very one who plugs poor Tom.

Now of course, this is manipulation to the nth power. But that's ok, lots of movies do that. But it is *not* ok here. And why?

Because it gives the lie to the great part of the film.

That wonderful twenty-four minute sequence? What did that tell us about war? That it is awful, yes, of course that. But it also told us this: **war is non-sensical, illogical, totally beyond human comprehension.**

But here it is all totally understandable. Let a bad guy go, guess what, he will return, relentless and helmetless to kill you. (And hang around conveniently so the cowardly lion of the flick, the translator, can become a man by killing the very man who shot his captain.) In order for this sequence to be in balance with the entire film, that opening battle sequence would have to be altered so that it was about John Wayne fighting his way to glory and saving all his raw recruits around him. Then this bullshit with the German soldier is in keeping with the film.

But it doesn't fucking matter who kills Tom Hanks. His death is what matters. His *death* is the tragedy.

The Death of Tom Hanks

Hanks is dying, Ed Burns runs for a medic, Matt Damon is alone with Hanks. And do you know what Hanks' last words were? Of course you don't, no one does, not the first time they see the movie. Because not only are they whispered so softly, they never before been spoken on this or any planet. "Earn this . . . earn it." Those are the words.

I have zero idea what that can possibly mean. My only explanation is this: Spielberg was up half the night before reading *Philosophy for Dummies* and he wanted to inject that nugget into his flick.

Ed Burns at the Cemetery

Hanks is dead, the awful pretentious voice of the actor playing General Marshall is treackling away, we hear ole Honest Abe's letter again and I am now waiting for the shot of Ed Burns with the big boobed girls back at the cemetery. Why do I know that is coming? Well, only two members of the squad are left, Burns and the cowardly translator and I know it can't be him because he was not with Hanks and the squad during the twenty-four minutes of glory at the start of the film. So it has to be Burns standing there among the graves.

Now the morphing shot comes—

—and I am looking at the old face of Matt Damon at the cemetery.

Well, you can't do that. **Don't you see, he wasn't fucking** **there.** He knew nothing of the attack on the beach, knew nothing of the odyssey that followed, and he never had a chance to hear about it. The only spare moment he had was when he was telling us all about his brothers and the ugly girl and setting the barn on fire.

When he was great, and he was great, Spielberg was a phenomenal storyteller. All gone. That, or he doesn't care.

How's about Spielberg's version of *Moby Dick*: "Call me Ishmael. I'm going to tell you story of this ship and this one legged captain and this whale. Actually, I don't know if the guy was one legged. Never saw him, never saw the ship, never saw the whale, never talked to anybody who ever saw anything.

"Who better than I to tell you what happened?"

The other disgrace of this storytelling is this: *there is no pregnant moment to the story.* (I'm not going all intellectual on you—remember, the Zipper scene and Matt Dillon trying to electrocute the dog back to life were my happiest moments this year in a theatre.) But all stories do and must have them. They are the reason the story is being told. The pregnant moment of *Shakespeare in Love* is this: Will has a block. We do not tell of Joe and Gwyneth after he's written *King Lear*—the whole point is the guy can't write anything. *Armageddon* happens when it happens *because the meteor is on it's way.*

There is absolutely no reason for this story being told now since Matt has no specific reason for visiting the cemetery.

Didn't have to be phony. Say it *was* Ed Burns. Who has the flashback legitimately. Say he had a reason for coming—

pick any one you want. Try this: Ryan has just done something splendid. Or Ryan has just died but had a good life.

"Remember that little shit you died for?" Burns might say. "Guess what? He turned out okay. Not worth your dying, Captain, but at least it's something. Thought you'd like to know."

The Ending

Just when you think Spielberg has stooped as low as even he can, new thresholds are reached. Four agonizing minutes of pretentious syrup, climaxing when Matt asks his wife has he been a good man? *What is she going to answer?* Her husband is clearly having a breakdown. She says yes and Matt—wait for it—he salutes!

Then Old Glory returns, waving at us for half a minute. I guess reminding us that God and Steven Spielberg are on the same side.

Medicinal Level—A.

Can't get much higher. Patriotism and the flag and easy answers galore. Phony and manipulative, all in the sense of Country.

What to say about Spielberg at this stage of his career? He will win his second Oscar for this work, and probably a third when he finds another 'importante' subject to hide behind. (Religious persecution, racial injustice, patriotism.)

I have never met him, never been in a room with him,

but no person can come so far in such a killingly competitive business without having a reservoir of anger and rage and darkness hiding in there somewhere. I just wish once he would let it show.

There is no reason for him to do anything else than what he has been doing. The movies are wildly successful at the box-office, the critics bow.

And if he had directed *Bambi*, guess what? Bambi's mother would never have died . . .

STUDIO OF THE DECADE

Miramax

With no other studio even close.

Amazing what the Brothers Weinstein have wrought. A decade back, they were nomads, wandering the movie deserts of the world, hoping to snare the rights to some pretentious Mongolian art film. Now they own the Oscars.

100 plus nominations this decade, (twenty-three this year.)

And sure, some of their stuff is still artsy-fartsy. But not *Good Will Hunting*, not *The English Patient* or *The Crying Game* or *Pulp Fiction* or *Scream* (the franchise.)

True, many of their greatest successes have been developed by other companies. True, when you are on a ride like theirs, ego can unbalance the act with shocking speed.

But I don't think their ride is over. They are by far the best in the business at selling. They are masters of hype.

Maybe their greatest advantage is who they're up against: ex-agents and Harvard Law graduates who don't much care about movies, who refer to them as 'product,' who can't spell the word 'quality,' who study just the bottom line.

Like the great moguls of the past the Weinsteins are not cuddly. They don't get ulcers, they give them. Their life is their work, they live above the store.

And they love film.

SHAKESPEARE IN LOVE

Marc Norman's idea provides the basis for, at best, a one joke show. The movie itself has bad jokes galore—may the earth turn forever with no more references to Ethel the Pirate Queen. There are two stupid swordfights, two too many. There is a dreadful ending that must have been tacked on from some other English flick. The entire Queen Elizabeth subplot is not needed, and could have been handed so much more skillfully than it is. So why is the movie so wonderful?

Because Norman's notion—Will has a block—is clever enough by half to sustain the piece and his screenplay—with help from Tom Stoppard—is wonderfully witty and surprising. (Not funny though. If it wins Best Picture it will go down as the least funny comedy ever to win.) The directing by John Madden is just about perfect and the acting, especially Geoffrey Rush as an addled producer—kind of sublime.

And no movie this decade is such a valentine to the theatre, to the poor greasepainted fools who come most alive when they can tromp around on a stage in the company of strangers.

It received the most nominations—a wonderful thirteen—so it should all be a tromp into the sunset. Ahhh, but. There is that little matter of plagiarism. I am writing this the day the nominations came out so the entire matter may blow up or disappear.

But the *New York Post*—I know, I know—reported on February 7th that the *London Evening Standard*—an absolutely respected rag—had run an article about a book entitled *No Bed For Bacon*. In that novel, the heroine, "Lady Viola, dresses herself as a boy in order to act on the London stage, where she falls in love with William Shakespeare. Shakespeare, in turn, is creatively inspired by the love affair."

And worst of all Tom Stoppard knew of the book. (It had been a gift from a friend.) Marc Norman, who had made up the story of *Shakespeare in Love*, knew nothing of the novel.

Should this matter?

Of course not.

But the Oscars are worth millions of dollars as well as lifetime prestige, so I can't imagine the story won't surface. And it could change a few votes. Miramax will do it's best to contain it, and if anybody can put a happy spin on things, they're the guys to do it.

I still cannot imagine this movie not winning honors. Judi Dench—one of the great living stage actresses, is up for *Elizabeth*—an eight minute job, which I know Miramax will turn into a plus. Screenplay could win, all those wonderful technicians that were nominated.

But Gwyneth Paltrow is the lock. For me, anyway.

And I wish someone would do a study of how many career making roles were turned down by other performers. Just last year, Helen Hunt only got the part in *As Good as It Gets* after Holly Hunter—for whom it was written—turned it down.

Shakespeare in Love was going to be Julia Roberts. I have no idea why she finally said "no" but her career sure hasn't suffered. I do think this: she would have won the Oscar too. So would Uma Thurman if she'd played it. Don't laugh, but I think Winona Rider would also have won. And Cate Blanchett. And Nicole Kidman would have been sensational. Not to mention literally scores of young British performers.

It's just a great part. You get to be a boy, you get to be a girl, you get to play passionate, you get to play heartbroken, you get to be witty and sexy and and and—you're not saving

Edgar Bronfman Jr. from destroying Universal, my god, *you're saving Shakespeare.*

Medicinal Level—A

To repeat: it's Shakespeare, folks. He makes us all feel like better human beings. If this movie had been called *Aeschylus in Love*, it would have grossed less than *Ishtar.*

PRODUCER OF THE DECADE

Scott Rudin

When I started into this madness, thirty five years ago, there were two great producers: Sam Spiegel, who seemed to produce a movie every decade, and Hal Wallis, who seemed to produce a decade's worth of movies every year. (Spiegel produced only 17 movies in a forty plus year career, over half of which won some kind of nomination, and three won Best Picture Awards. Wallis won twice but produced *nineteen* other movies that were nominated for Best Picture. Yes, you read that right.)

Scott Rudin hasn't won Best Picture yet but he's young. This year he had *The Truman Show* and *A Civil Action*. Like Wallis, he produces all kinds of stuff. (Wallis had *Beckett* and an Elvis flick in the same year.) This decade Rudin has produced, among many others, and in no particular order, *Flatliners*, *Regarding Henry*, *Addams Family* (and the sequel), *Nobody's Fool*, *Little Man Tate*, *Sister Act* (and the sequel), *Searching for Bobby Fisher*, *The Firm*, *Clueless*, *In and Out*, *The First Wives' Club*, *Ransom*.

Since he has so much time on his hands, he is also one of the busier theatrical producers both in New York and London. Just forty, he is going to have one of the legendary careers—providing his heart holds up. (Rudin is not known for suffering fools, either quietly or well.)

LIFE IS BEAUTIFUL

This year's entrant in the Holocaust derby, and, in a little way, almost as controversial as *Saving Private Ryan.* By which I mean a lot of people adore this film, wept buckets as it unwound. A lot of others thought it was trivializing the Holocaust. There were great moments here, no question.

But ultimately, I didn't believe it, not for a New York minute.

The first scene has two goofy guys zooming down a country road in a crummy car. (We have already heard in voice over that what we are about to see is a simple story but not an easy one to tell. A fable.) OK, the brakes fail in the car, the vehicle veers off the road and through woods, ultimately coming out safely on the road again. Two motorcycles appear on the road just ahead of it. A voice says this: *the King is coming.*

A small village has gathered on both sides of the road. They are there to see their King. Roberto Benigni, one of the goofy guys—also the writer, director, and star of the whole deal—stands up in the car and shouts to the villagers that their brakes have failed. He gestures wildly, sometimes accidently doing a Fascist salute.

And guess what? The villagers gives him the Fascist salute right back as his car sails safely through. Pause. Now the real King comes—bearing no resemblance to Benigni any more than his grand car does to the brakeless jalopy. And people just look kind of strangely at their ruler.

In other words, these people have no idea who their king is.

Is this possible? Yes, certainly—*before the invention of the camera. But this is Italy. 1939.*

I started going for the exit in my head right there.

Roberto Benigni's idea is this: a father and son are taken to a concentration camp, stuck in a barracks with a lot of other men. And in a wonderful act of love, Benigni makes up a game of the whole thing—the one who first gets to a thousand points wins a tank.

All to save his child from terror and madness.

Benigni was not well known here until this movie—but he is a giant comedy star in the rest of the world. And this movie, though not as farcical as some of his other work, is still not meant to be taken as realistically say as a Scorsese flick.

Still, for any kind of world you set up in a movie, there are rules. The authors of the film make the rules—and they break them at their peril.

OK, we are in the barracks—a concentration camp barracks—despair, smells, all those neat things. Now, some guards come in to give instructions to the new arrivals—

—and not one of all those Italian men speaks German—hello?—

—so Benigni jumps up and translates, going on with *his* private game with his kid. He talks of such things as lollipops. I don't know about you, but I would have been terrified in that barracks and desperate not make a mistake. None of these guys though. They just stand there.

But that was only the beginning. I have been with groups of men. I think most men have been with groups of men—in school, playing sports, in the service, on and on.

And as the days in the camp went by, as Benigni kept

going on and on to his kid about the tank game, all I could think of was this: why didn't someone go up to him and say—"SHUT UP. Stop with your stupid tank game. We are going to die and we know it."

Or, someone could have come up to Benigni and the kid and said this: "you know, last month I thought my son—he's just in the barracks across the way—I thought he was going to win the tank. I would have bet anything on it, but then he started crying one day and they took points away from him. I think, Benigni, your kid has a wonderful shot at winning if he just doesn't cry."

In other words, they don't have to hate him—they can try and help him—but they have to take some kind of notice of what is going on. Attention must be paid.

Medicinal level—A

If I gave an A-plus, this one would get it. The Holocaust alone almost does it. Then throw in families who's love is deep and endless and perfect. (Note: since Holocaust flicks are almost as hot as asteroid flicks, my two cents. Check out a documentary called, *George Stevens, A Filmmakers Journey*. Stevens, the most underrated of the great directors, was among the first to shoot the Holocaust in color. His shots of the bodies stacked up like cordwood in the camps, with blood smeared everyplace, are real and almost too haunting. For me, shooting this material in black and white removes you from the horror. And is total horseshit.)

DIRECTOR OF THE DECADE

James Cameron, alas.

Nothing more clearly indicates the sad level of 90's films than Cameron's name here. For example, if I were picking the director of the 70's, my answer would be Francis Ford Coppola, whose four flicks were *Godfathers I* and *II, The Conversation* and *Apocalypse Now*. Cameron's trio of *Terminator 2: Judgment Day, True Lies* and *Titanic* simply do not match up.

Still, not chopped liver.

The first two were world wide successes and *Titanic*, though it never found much of an audience, is clearly a film— some dialogue aside—of quality.

This is the age of special effects. And Cameron is as good as the game. You may argue with the kind of story he chooses to turn his talents to, but his talents are genuine, his storytelling instincts usually sound.

And I think he's going to get better. Why do I think that? Because he *was* better. *Aliens* is on the very short list of films about which you can argue that the sequel was at least as good as the original. And *Terminator* would make my list of the very best of the 80's.

I hated his repulsive performance Oscar night. But I'll be in line the day his next film opens, popcorn in hand.

ELIZABETH

This year's history lesson or, Masterpiece Theatre rides again.

Lot of good stuff here. Well produced, deserved all the technical nominations it received. And Cate Blanchett as the Virgin Queen, really is something. You can see her grow and change and sadden.

And I liked this movie by far least of the five.

Because of the direction.

When I'm sitting out there in the dark, all I want is for you to tell me a wonderful story. In that hour of *Saving Private Ryan*, when Spielberg has his troops under Hanks on their odyssey, I'm in heaven.

And I am not aware of anything special.

Rodat's script was fine and the acting was fine and of course the direction and all the other technicians that work so killingly hard to try and tell the story, they were fine. They were this wonderfully grooved unit. Which to me, is what good storytelling is.

In this movie, *Elizabeth*, the director—named Shekhar Kapur—would not stop ruining things. I quit counting after awhile but there were at least twenty shots *that came from the ceiling*. I never saw the top of so many good actor's heads.

And he would never just let two actors just stand there and *act*. His camera kept moving pointlessly, every set-up was framed to call attention to itself, *not* what was going on. And I doubt there was an unrented smoke machine in all of England.

I once got the chance to interview one of the greatest of all cinematographers, Gordon Willis—*The Godfathers, All the*

President's Men, Annie Hall, etc etc. (Never won the Oscar, folks. Amazing.) Anyway, this is what he said to me: "Often, the trick on a movie is to take something that's often very sophisticated and reduce it to something very simple. That's hard, because not too many people understand simplicity: They equate it with 'no good.' "

There is no question that Kapur is talented. But right now, instead of directing a movie he is jumping in front of the camera, waving his arms and shouting, "Look at me, everybody, I'm the star."

I really would have liked the chance to see this movie. But Kapur stopped that from happening. I hope he changes. (I know I'm too old to.) If he does, could be a terrific career. If not, it's another case of stop me before I kill more.

Medicinal Level—A minus.

English history, natch; that's always healthy for us heathen colonists. Plus this: feminism. I am woman, hear me roar.

STAR OF THE DECADE

Tom Hanks

If you had predicted, in 1990, that Tom Hanks was going to be, well, Tom Hanks, you would have been carted off to Bellevue. His prior three movies had been *The 'Burbs, Turner and Hooch*, and, the bottom of anybody's pit, *The Bonfire of the Vanities*.

In '93, he caught fire and these are his last six starring movies-*Sleepless in Seattle, Philadelphia, Forrest Gump, Apollo 13, Saving Private Ryan, You've Got Mail*. There have been few better streaks in movie history.

Some say he is our Jimmy Stewart. They are wrong. Others say he is our Spencer Tracy. Wrong again.

A young writer said recently he could only assume the true greatness of Marlon Brando, because *he wasn't there* when Brando was great. He could *appreciate*, say, that Brando was giving a great performance in *On the Waterfront*. He could *learn* in books the historical importance of that performance. But he could only take the *shock* of the young Brando on faith.

In decades to come, people will look at Hanks work in, say, *Philadelphia*, and have to take the shock of his work on faith. *They weren't there.*

But we are here, right now, as Hanks' career unfolds. We can watch what he tries next, and the time after the next time. He is our Tom Hanks, and sometimes things do work out for the best.

THE THIN RED LINE

The Thin Red Line is about nature, Mother and Human.

There is wonderful stuff throughout. The best performance of Nick Nolte's career, fabulous cinematography by John Toll, brilliant scenes, both on the phone and in person, between Nolte and Elias Koteas as the Greek American Captain. Better nature shots than any ten documentaries you might mention. And riding over it all, the intelligence of Terence Malick, who adapted the James Jones novel and, after twenty years, turned his hand back to directing.

Malick—for all his brilliance, has always had a problem—story. And here, the story he chose to tell, is the problem. Because this was a movie more admired than loved.

It's hard to know what was in Malick's head—the movie has obviously been enormously altered from whatever he began with. George Clooney appears for the first time two and a half *hours* into the flick and is on camera for less than a *minute*.

There is a nine minute opening sequence involving some men who have gone AWOL. The story really begins fifteen minutes in, when Travolta—in another tiny part—talks to Nolte.

This is a weird heffalump of a piece. And what keeps it going is you haven't seen anything quite like it. And my feeling is that of all the Best Picture nominees, *The Thin Red Line* drew the fewest votes.

And now is as good a time as any to put in my annual plea—*let us know the votes, for God's sakes.* How close did Blanchett come to Paltrow? Did the four art film guys cancel each other out and leave a clear field for Hanks? Wouldn't you like to know this kind of thing? I sure would. But the Academy, for reasons unknown to man, will never do such a thing.

And I would love to know how the Academy treated this splendid effort. It did not do much business for a movie this expensive and with so many stars. People didn't "get" it. And I think if he had begun the movie with Travolta and Nolte and ended it when the hill was finally conquered, it might have been enormously successful.

But would Malick have been happy? Strange figure, who knows. But I hope he directs again before 2020. And I hope he can look back at this effort in years to come and say "yeah, I did that."

Medicinal Level—C

The lowest of the five by far. All it tells us is that war is non-sensical, illogical, totally beyond human comprehension. What *Saving Private Ryan* told us for twenty four minutes—before God and country took command.

WHAT KIND OF YEAR HAS IT BEEN?

I just want to say one word to you . . . Cassettes!

Paraphrasing that wonderful line from *The Graduate* seems as good a way as any to explain the nominations. And not just for now. I believe this much is clear:

The Oscars will never be the same.

Not necessarily a bad thing. The Academy has been goofing for decades. But I think it's fair to say that if cassettes had existed before, all kinds of movies would have been honored that were overlooked before. *The Killing, Ride the High Country, This is Spinal Tap, Mean Streets, Body Heat.*

The Academy simply did not see them. The members are not all brimmng with youthful vitality (full disclosure: I am 67) and not adventurous and what cassettes do is let them see movies they would never remotely have ventured out of the house for. How else do you account for Ed Norton getting a deserved nomination for *American History X*? According to my Feb 8-14 issue of *Variety, Affliction* has grossed $599,615. Could they *all* have been Nick Nolte fans?

So the Oscars are a different game. Not a better one, incidentally. My favorite this year is Best Make-Up. Only three movies nominated. Think a minute. *Elizabeth.* That's one. Think again. *Shakespeare in Love,* that's two.

Who got the third Best Make-Up nomination?

Think, dammit. It's so obvious. It's the greatest make-up work since Lon Chaney Sr. packed it in. Got it?

Ok—wait for it—*Saving Private Ryan!* I don't know about you, but when I left that flick I did not talk about the brilliant twenty-four minutes of bloodshed. Nosiree. It was the make-up that rocked me. (This is not to belittle those technicians—they did a terrific job. But still . . .) So who's gonna win?

The Academy goes for sweeps and only two movies can do that.

Saving Private Ryan and Kremlinologist that I am, I am going back to the make-up nomination. My God, the respect for the flick must run amazingly deep, so maybe it will sweep. But—it did not get any supporting actor nominations. Tom Sizemore, among others, was passed over. So maybe the respect isn't that deep after all. (See why we need to know the votes?)

Shakespeare in Love won everything it was supposed to. Could it sweep? Not if the plagiarism madness haunts it. Not if *Elizabeth* cuts into it's vote, which is certainly could.

Personally, I do not think the Academy can deny Steven Spielberg the directing award. He wants it too much, has a great hype machine going, is too powerful and makes too much money for too many studios. Plus this: some of his work is as good as anything he's ever done.

So could he win director and *Ryan* not win picture? Possible. Happened before. Will it this year? *That* is what we we will waiting for come the 21st of March.

Paltrow has to win. It's her time. And she was wonderful. But for me, the best performance this year male or female was Fernanda Montenegro in *Central Station*. Not unlike Giulietta Masina's work in *Nights of Caberia*.

I am shocked at the relative ignoring of *The Truman Show*. A major star giving not just a wonderful performance but a *different* performance. An inventive and different movie that grossed over 125 million. That got great reviews. That's what used to win before the attack of the killer cassettes.

There's Something About Mary gave me more pleasure than anything else. While the rest of you are undergoing English history with Cate Blanchett or Robert Benigni's winking at the camera or Matt Damon, a tremblin' as he salutes Ole Glory, I think I'll just watch watch Cameron Diaz inviting Ben Stiller up to watch *SportsCenter*. Or maybe it'll be the zipper scene again. No, I'll take a look at Matt Dillon electrocuting the dog.

So many choices, so little time . . .

—APRIL 1999

THE FOLLOWING WERE ACADEMY AWARD WINNERS FOR 1998:

Best Actor	*Roberto Benigni, Life is Beautiful*
Best Actress	*Gwyneth Paltrow, Shakespeare in Love*
Best Director	*Steven Spielberg, Saving Private Ryan*
Best Picture	*Shakespeare in Love*

BIKINI SHOPPING WITH ELIZABETH HURLEY

It was just your ordinary Friday by the pool at the Hotel duCap until Elizabeth Hurley said, "Bill, would you like to go bikini shopping with me this afternoon?"

Probably most of you get lots of invitations like that. More than likely, you're bored doing stuff like that. But since most of my life is spent alone in my pit, it seemed new and different. You will be shocked — shocked — to learn I said I would indeed try to somehow find the time to tag along.

We took a cab into Juan-les-pain, the Brigadoon-like place on the Riviera that only exists during tourist season, alighted from the vehicle, started our search. I have known Hurley for several years, was around *Extreme Measures*, a movie she produced, (yes, she really is up early,) and find her pretty enchanting. She's bright and funny and eats a lot; something which is close to my heart. When we met, she was just this girl-friend of this English guy who had exploded with *Four Weddings and a Funeral*. Now she's a celebrity all on her lonesome. Not a giant star perhaps, except in England. But hers is one of the famous faces, no question.

No one pestered us as we made our way to the shop she hoped would answer her needs. Blumarine. Tiny, narrow. We went in, she found the bikini department — a large wicker basket — began rummaging through. I took a seat close to the action.

A couple of middle-aged women came in, checked out some dresses, shook their heads, glanced at Elizabeth without recognition, left. Elizabeth, torn between two bikini's, selected one, moved to the back of the shop to look at some summer dresses.

Another couple came in, a teen-aged girl and her mum — checked out the merchandise, checked out who else was in the shop — which was when the teen-ager did what all people do when they recognize a celebrity — *they spin*. Either their heads or their body or their arms — but invariably they move faster than they usually do. Faster than anybody usually does.

The teen ager spun toward her mother, elbowed her in the ribs, nodded her head sharply toward Elizabeth. The mother recognized her too, they exchanged glances, then moved awkwardly toward the rear of the shop, idly fumbling at merchandise while they stared.

And sitting there watching I realized this: most people never see a famous face. Most people live their lives with others who are only recognizable on their block of life. And fame does strange things to them when they encounter it.

I have been with a lot of famous people over the decades — it is never much fun — trust me please — and I know only this: very few of them can deal with it.

I have never met Sylvester Stallone but I will always remember the first time I saw him. Maybe a decade past. In the dining room of the Carlyle Hotel in New York, at a business breakfast I was having with an agent.

Two things you must know: 1) it was probably the only business breakfast of my life and 2) The Carlyle Hotel dining room at such an hour is the reverse of Times Square on New Year's Eve. Dead silent. My memory of the people eating there was that the average age might be eighty, wealthy widows and their money managers.

It is an elegant room, one of the city's prettiest and suddenly I was aware of a commotion at the door — I glanced up and saw four HUGE guys in I think white summer suits.

Like a circus attraction that was very much lost.

Then I saw this *very* ordinary sized guy wedged among them. The biggest of the HUGE guys muttered something to the effect that they needed a place where they would be safe and not bothered. The maitre d' escorted them to a quiet distant corner and as I watched them cross the room, I wondered what in the world did he need those HUGE guys for?

At a premiere, sure. At a Planet Hollywood opening, oh absolutely. But here, in the most discreet dining room in the city? *Nobody knew who he was*, don't you see? He was generations too young for their memories. Jimmy Stewart they would have known. Maybe even a squirt like Jack Lemmon. But a muscle star barely forty?

I guess they ensured, for him, his fame. My God, he must have told himself. I *must* be somebody special — shit, I'm the only one around needs bodyguards to eat grapefruit safely.

In Blumarine now, the mom and daughter combo where flanking Hurley, who was deciding between which of several red summer dresses were preferable. She must have been aware of the silent attention. But she concentrated on her task, let them stare all they wanted.

The star I have worked with it who deals with fame best is Eastwood. (Though Schwarzenegger and Newman are right up there.) I was visiting the set of *Absolute Power* when it was shooting in Baltimore. Lunch break. The shooting was in a museum and lunch was a block away, in an empty store the company had rented for the duration of the stay and turned into a cafeteria.

Eastwood exited the museum where a car was waiting to drive him the block. He shook his head, crossed the street, started alone up the sidewalk. I followed. (I do that. I once saw

Jimmy Cagney get off *the crosstown bus* on East 57th street and start walking with a friend. I forget what I was doing there but whatever it was, nothing on earth was as important to me right then as following that man in the flesh, with that walk, the lilt, the whole great package.)

Anyway, there is Clint on the Baltimore sidewalk, lunch hour, people streaming past him. Me half a dozen steps behind. Now this thing starts to happen. A real life double-take. Numberless Baltimoreans move past this lone mid-sixties guy. No reaction. Another step. They look at each other, start to say something like, probably, 'that guy remind you of...?'

Nawww.

Another step. Now they are staring at each other, turning quickly back. Then they stop.

Dead on the sidewalk.

Holy shit.

Then they spin.

It's *him*. He's *here*. Dirty Harry walks amongst us.

Back they all scurry and he is gracious, always that, soft spoken, that too, and he nods to them and smiles back at them and if they give him something to sign, why, of course, he signs it —

— but he never stops walking. They would have had him then.

He reaches the cafeteria, nods courteously a final time, then goes inside, gets in line for his tray —

— let me say that again for those of you new to the entertainment business — *he gets in line for his tray* — waits in line for his food, then goes to a table and has his meal, just like anybody else.

What has kept him on top all these decades — the most durable star in the history of sound — is that somehow he has clung to this truth: that in spite of his fame, in spite of our millions of spins toward him, that he *is* just like anybody else.

Back in Blumarine now, the mother glances at her teenager indicates they must leave. A look of such pain on the teenager's face. 'Leave? *Leave now? You're destroying my life*!!!!' Mum takes her arm, all business, and they are gone.

Hurley finishes her shopping, takes her stuff to the saleslady, gives her a credit card. In the front I stand, stretch, the adventure coming to an end. Then I hear Hurley saying, "I was just in London, it worked there."

Now the saleslady — who clearly has heard this song before — mutters that perhaps she might have another credit card. Hurley gets out her second card.

Ngggggg!

I start wandering back. Hurley is confused, a bit flustered, takes out her last card, hands it over to the unsmiling saleslady who is really quite nice and clearly has zero idea of who was trying to buy, among other things, a bikini.

No good. None of her credit cards work. A bit desperate now, Hurley manages this: "Perhaps it's your machine."

The Saleslady, increasingly distrustful at this point, is having none of it. "It is a new machine." she says. Firmly.

"Problem?" I enquire.

"My credit cards won't work," Hurley says to me. "But they all worked yesterday, I swear," She looks at me, blue eyes irresistible.

"Allow me," say I. Boyer was never more suave.

Now, I have two credit cards with me, one an ordinary

one I use a lot, which sometimes won't work in Europe, because I'm overdrawn, especially when plane tickets are involved. My other, my fastball, is a platinum baby that I *never* use, so that way I know I *can't* be overdrawn. I give her my crummy card.

The machine rejects it out so fast you wouldn't believe it. I turn to Hurley. "It worked yesterday," I say. "Mine too," Hurley replies.

But that's four out of four and we are preaching to the converted, and the saleslady is clearly beginning to believe this is all a scam. "Perhaps you can pick this up later," she says, indicating the small bag of clothing.

"Ridiculous," I tell her, whipping out my platinum job. It glistens it is so virginal. In it goes.

The machine vomits it out.

"Are you sure your putting them in the right way?" Elizabeth asks helpfully.

The saleslady tries flipping it, jamming it back in. Nope.

Then she crams it in the original way again — and yes Lord, it is accepted! We all sigh, smile, Elizabeth starts to sign before she realizes it is my card she is signing. I sign, we wish the saleslady the best, and off we go into the sunlight, virtue triumphant.

That night there was a message for me — my beloved unused platinum had been *voided*. Suspicious dealings of some sort or another. They left a number for me to call. I called. Got a lovely young woman who worked at a small computer company in Northern California. I apologized, dialed again, got her again, got her a third time. The credit card company had given me the wrong number.

I understood — when you get to go bikini shopping with one of God's creatures, you must be humbled, lest arrogance set in. Feeling very humble indeed. I tried, unsuccessfully, to sleep, trying to prepare myself for the less glamourous days of my life that were certain to be ahead.

The bikini was white. Size 38 or 4, depending on country. There. Now you know everything...

THE GHOST AND THE DARKNESS
WILLIAM GOLDMAN

ONLY THE MOST INCREDIBLE PARTS OF THE STORY ARE TRUE.

"THE RARE HOLLYWOOD ACTION-ADVENTURE THAT BECOMES MORE SURPRISING AND EXOTIC AS IT MOVES ALONG...NAIL-BITING TENSION." —Janet Maslin, THE NEW YORK TIMES

"SPELLBINDING...SPECTACULAR. AN INCREDIBLE STORY." —Jack Mathews, NEWSDAY

"A HEART-POUNDING, WHITE-KNUCKLE ADVENTURE! A THRILLER OF A NAIL-BITER — LEAVES YOU BREATHLESS! DON'T MISS!" —Bonnie Churchill, NATIONAL NEWS SYNDICATE

"A HYPNOTIC SPECTACLE." —Peter Travers, ROLLING STONE

$14.95 • PAPER • ISBN 1-55783-267-6

A FISH CALLED WANDA

by John Cleese and Charles Crichton

*"The **FUNNIEST** movie this year!"*
— ROGER EBERT,
SISKEL & EBERT

"Wanda defies gravity, in both senses of the work, and
REDEFINES A GREAT COMIC TRADITION."
— RICHARD SCHICKEL, *TIME*

*"**WANDA** is wonderful ... I fell for it hook, line and
sinker. The script is **HYSTERICAL.**"*
— JOEL SIEGEL, ABC–TV

*"The **MEANEST,** most consistently hysterical film in
ages ... the writing is sharply pointed and delightfully
irreverent."*
— MARSHALL FINE
GANNETT NEWSPAPERS

"OUTRAGEOUSLY OUTSTANDING!"
— DENNIS CUNNINGHAM, CBS–TV

1-55783-033-9 • Paperback • $8.95

MICHAEL CAINE
ACTING IN FILM
An Actor's Take on Movie Making

Academy Award winning actor Michael Caine, internationally acclaimed for his talented performances in movies for over 25 years, reveals secrets for success on screen. *Acting in Film* is also available on video (the BBC Master Class).

"Michael Caine knows the territory...*Acting in Film* is wonderful reading, even for those who would not dream of playing 'Lets Pretend' in front of a camera. Caine's guidance, aimed at novices still dreaming of the big break, can also give hardened critics fresh insights to what it is they're seeing up there on the screen..."
—Charles Champlin, LOS ANGELES TIMES

"FASCINATING! Wonderfully practical film acting wisdom—all put across in the best Caine style."
—John Cleese

BOOK/PAPER: $14.95• ISBN: 1-55783-277-3
VIDEO: $29.95 • ISBN: 1-55783-034-7

WILLIAM GOLDMAN
FIVE SCREENPLAYS
WITH ESSAYS

ALL THE PRESIDENT'S MEN
Academy Award® Winner
"...**RIVETING SCREEN ADAPTATION** by William Goldman...a breathtaking adventure...an unequivocal smash-hit—the thinking man's *Jaws*."
—Vincent Canby, *THE NEW YORK TIMES*

HARPER
"**GOLDMAN'S SCRIPT CRACKLES, SNAPS AND POPS** with all sorts of familiar surprised and bubbles of biting dialogue." —*THE NEW YORK TIMES*

THE GREAT WALDO PEPPER
"Screenwriter William Goldman characteristically cooks up **ONE CLEVER REVERSAL OF EXPECTATIONS AFTER ANOTHER** to keep his lightweight vehicle airborne."
—*NEWSWEEK*

MAGIC
"AN ATMOSPHERIC THRILLER . . . **AN ABSORBING CHARACTER STUDY**." —*VARIETY*

MAVERICK
"Fast, funny and full of straight ahead action and tongue-in-cheek jokes...a smart, new-fangled Maverick."
—Caryn James, THE NEW YORK TIMES

CLOTH • ISBN 1-55783-266-8
PAPER • ISBN 1-55783-362-1

WILLIAM GOLDMAN FOUR SCREENPLAYS

William Goldman, master craftsman and two-time Oscar winner continues his irreverent analysis with merciless essays written expressly for this landmark edition of his screen work. Nobody covers the psychic and political terrain behind the Hollywood lot with more cynical wisdom and practical savvy than the much celebrated author of ADVENTURES IN THE SCREEN TRADE.

William Goldman won Academy Awards for BUTCH CASSIDY AND THE SUNDANCE KID and ALL THE PRESIDENT'S MEN

Includes the screenplays:

BUTCH CASSIDY AND THE SUNDANCE KID

THE PRINCESS BRIDE

MARATHON MAN

MISERY

PAPER • ISBN 1-55783-265-X
CLOTH • ISBN 1-55783-198-X